SINGAPORE
PERSPECTIVES 2013
Governance

SINGAPORE
PERSPECTIVES 2013
Governance

Edited by

Gillian Koh
Institute of Policy Studies, Singapore

LKY Lee Kuan Yew
School of Public Policy
National University of Singapore

iPS Institute of
Policy Studies

World Scientific

Published by

World Scientific Publishing Co. Pte. Ltd.

5 Toh Tuck Link, Singapore 596224

USA office: 27 Warren Street, Suite 401-402, Hackensack, NJ 07601

UK office: 57 Shelton Street, Covent Garden, London WC2H 9HE

British Library Cataloguing-in-Publication Data

A catalogue record for this book is available from the British Library.

SINGAPORE PERSPECTIVES 2013
Governance

ISBN 978-981-4520-74-4 (pbk)

In-house Editor: Sandhya Venkatesh

Contents

Preface

When the date of the Singapore Perspectives Conference 2013 was fixed on 28 January 2013, there was no inkling of what might take place before it. As fate would have it, the conference was the first large-scale public interest gathering since the governing party, the People's Action Party (PAP), was defeated in the Punggol East by-election held two days before — thus the full-court press attendance at the event. Be that as it may, the conference had been in the making for more than year, being the culmination of a scenario planning exercise we undertook, dubbed "IPS Prism".

The exercise posed a simple question: "How will we govern ourselves in 2022?" — in essence, two election cycles from now. It sought to engage the public on their views of the future of governance in Singapore.

When the idea of such a project was first proposed, I was initially sceptical. Unlike in large organisations that use the scenario planning method, the people involved in IPS Prism would have little in common aside from their citizenship. Would a group of people who did not share a similar set of assumptions be able to meet fruitfully on this question, I wondered.

I was eventually assured that in a scenario planning exercise, the process is just as important as the outcome. The mere act of bringing together 140 people from a variety of sectors and demographic profiles — business, civil society, the arts and media, young Singaporeans, new citizens, academia and public service — to consider the most important question that citizens in a representative democracy could ask themselves, would be productive and of value in itself. This would be even more so when the larger public got involved. It would be an act of shaping political culture in Singapore.

Elections, it has been said, are means for people in democracies to have conversations among themselves. *Vox populi, vox dei* — sometimes the *vox* can sound like a bark, but it is speech nevertheless. The scenario planning exercise we conducted was a conversation about what that conversation would or should turn on: What will be the chief forces shaping our future? How shall we arrange ourselves to secure the best outcomes for ourselves as a country?

"If men were angels, no government would be necessary," wrote James Madison in The Federalist Papers. "If angels were to govern men, neither external nor internal controls on government would be necessary. In framing a government which is to be administered by men over men, the great difficulty lies in this: you must first enable the government to control the governed; and in the next place oblige it to control itself."

Humankind has been having this conversation about the conversation for some centuries now. In a humble way, IPS Prism was a tiny slipstream in that long conversation: Not being angels, how do we govern ourselves? Not being angels, how do we govern the governors?

As it turned out, both the process and the outcome were useful.

I will only make very brief comments here about the three scenarios that emerged in the first part of IPS Prism: the first is what we called "SingaStore.com", where there is strong government, Singapore is pro-business, and there is minimal but market-reinforcing social support provided by the state to the people. The second is called "SingaGives.gov", where there is also strong government, extensive social support and quality, inclusive growth. Finally, the third is called "Wikicity.sg", where government is weak and provides the people minimal social support, but there are strong community-based apparatuses where the spirit of self-help prevails.

One way to understand the three scenarios would be to make a distinction between the strength and scope of government. Governments can be weak or strong. Also, governments can have a wide or narrow scope; they can do a great deal or little. For example, the United States has a strong government — it can enforce laws effectively and conduct wars around the world — but its scope is relatively narrow. Compared to the Scandinavian countries, with their cradle-to-grave welfare systems, the US government does not provide extensive social support. SingaStore is strong government with narrow scope; SingaGives is strong government with extensive scope; and WikiCity is weak government with narrow scope.

Singaporeans will have to decide what permutation and combination of these various alternatives we want. These may not necessarily be mutually exclusive — each of these scenarios is not a hermetically sealed option in any event — although some combinations do not seem possible. For example, it is not possible to have a weak government with extensive scope.

But all this is of the future, "the Emergent". It would do us some good to look back and remember that the first scenario our founding political leaders developed turned out to be totally wrong. What did the seven men, who began gathering in the basement dining room of No. 38 Oxley Road 60 years ago to plan the establishment of the PAP, assume was the future of Singapore?

They all assumed Singapore had no future for they thought this island was an inextricable part of Malaya. And they were not the only ones. The Communist Party of Malaya too assumed that Singapore was a part of Malaya. Nobody — not the communists, not the non-communists, not the British, not the Malayans, not Mr Lee Kuan Yew, hardly anyone — assumed that Singapore could exist as a sovereign, independent state.

As we now know, they all turned out to be wrong. It is very important to remember this: that the chief architects of modern Singapore began with the assumption that Singapore was not viable. They were surprised to become Singaporeans. They all assumed they were something else: Malayans.

So remember this thing that is so easy to forget: Our founding fathers got their founding scenario wrong. They tripped over a fantasy — the merger with Malaya — and stumbled into reality: independent Singapore.

This remembrance is an occasion for humility. We can but spy through a glass darkly, and even the best of us often fail in our foresight. We get things wrong.

Our founding leaders had better luck with their second scenario: Singapore as a global city. It was Mr S. Rajaratnam who first gave voice to this scenario, as far back as 1972, decades before "globalisation" became a buzzword. It was a piece of remarkable foresight. (And if I may indulge myself in an aside, we have many scenario planning units in Singapore now, but not a single one, as far as I know, has come up with a scenario as powerfully formative for Singapore as Rajaratnam did that day in 1972 as he banged away on his typewriter, imagining Singapore as a global city.)

What he foresaw is today a reality. We live by connecting ourselves to a network of other global cities. We have, I suppose, arrived. Or have we?

I just want to suggest one thought here: Is it possible that we may have reached the limit of Rajaratnam's vision? Is it possible that we have to re-adjust our relationship to globalisation in order to remain Singaporean?

Singapore is both a city and a country. There is no other city of a comparable size anywhere in the world that is also a country. Unlike New York City, we do not have upstate New York; unlike London, we do not have the Home Counties. This country is its city. We are a country in a city.

What does that mean? It means many things, but among them this: this global city, open to the world, must also be a village, a haven from the world. All life exists in a particular time and place or it cannot exist at all. We can function globally, economically, financially, geo-politically, even intellectually, but we can only live and exist, locally. The "heartland" as we call it, cannot be at a global crossroads like Shenton Way.

Is it not true that many of the problems we face today — from housing prices to immigration, from work-life balance to stressful schools, from the widening income gap to emerging social divides — are a reflection of the fact that we are a global city as well as a country? How can we be both — global as well as local, a city as well as a village, cosmopolitan as well as thoroughly Singaporean — and make that difficult combination work?

We hear much of a new social compact. I suspect we have to have a new country-city, local-global compact.

We may be forgiven if we think governance is a matter of institutions and laws, agencies and procedures. It is, but it is not only those things. As we consider the theme of this book, I leave you with some stanzas from a poem by H.W. Longfellow called "The Builders". The poem has been something of a mantra for me through IPS Prism. Longfellow writes of how in ancient times, craftsmen were so diligent that they would take as much care crafting the unseen parts of cathedrals and churches as they would the seen parts. We have to take as much care with the unseen parts of governance — call it ideals, values, courage, whatever — as we do the seen.

Preface

In the elder days of Art,
Builders wrought with greatest care
Each minute and unseen part;
For the Gods see everywhere.

Let us do our work as well,
Both the unseen and the seen;
Make the house, where Gods [or Singaporeans] may dwell,
Beautiful, entire, and clean.

Janadas Devan

Director, Institute of Policy Studies
National University of Singapore

Acknowledgements

IPS is grateful to the following institutions for their support of Singapore Perspectives 2013 held on Monday, 28 January 2013.

Made possible by

Keppel Corporation

45 YEARS
Shaping the Future

TEMASEK

Supported by

HILL+KNOWLTON
STRATEGIES

HOUSING &
DEVELOPMENT
BOARD

ITE
Institute of Technical Education

KPMG
cutting through complexity

MPA
SINGAPORE

NYP NANYANG
THE INNOVATIVE POLYTECHNIC

NANYANG
TECHNOLOGICAL
UNIVERSITY

NUS
National University
of Singapore

NGEE ANN
POLYTECHNIC

PHILIPS

Supported by

Introduction

Singapore Perspectives 2013 was held on 28 January 2013, the start of the Institute of Policy Studies' 25th year of existence. At this quarter-century edition of its flagship conference, it was befitting that the theme turned to the *raison d'être* of the Institute — governance in Singapore.

The British cultural historian, Raymond Williams, described a cultural system as being composed at any one time of a set of relations among residual, dominant and emergent forms — the "residual" being practices "effectively formed in the past, but still active" in the present; the "dominant" being the effectively pre-eminent "system of meaning and values" governing lives now; and the "emergent" being "the new meanings and values, new practices, new relationships" that are being created.

Applying this tripartite system of analysis to governance in Singapore, the conference examined Singapore's political history and its bearing on governance today. Political history has had an imprint on the culture of governance as Singaporeans understand it. The two speakers in the first section of the conference and therefore contributors to this book, "The Residual", very ably provided an appreciation of some of the central principles of governance that must surely continue to guide politics and policy-making. These include the tolerance for diversity in a multi-racial, multi-religious and multi-lingual society; meritocracy; an open economy; the revulsion against corruption; and the high premium on law and order. The speakers also highlighted the deep societal changes that have precipitated shifts in political culture, where a better-educated populace has come to value political participation and competition much more than ever. "Thinking the unthinkable", one of the speakers provides three scenarios of political change in Singapore that could emerge over the next decade as a result of that trend.

The second section of the conference then turned to "The Dominant" — the structures and processes of governance that are currently in play, and how they respond to the growing complexity of our society and economy in the transition from a fast-growing industralised nation to a developed mature economy with a more active citizenry. The speakers highlighted the moves to modify the following: how the government relates to citizens; its role in economic development; the social compact to take greater heed of questions of distributional justice; and the ideal of "meritocracy" that is tempered by an equal focus on social mobility. Acting Minister for Culture, Community and Youth, Mr Lawrence Wong was quick to emphasise the need, however, to ensure that the participative democracy that is emerging in Singapore continues to be a "problem-solving democracy" and not otherwise. Their views are recorded in the second section of this book.

The third section of the conference turned to a discussion of the shape of things to come — "The Emergent". What new meanings, values, practices and relationships among government, business, civil society and citizens might emerge in the next decade? The outcomes of a year-long project called IPS Prism were presented. These included the IPS Prism Scenarios as well as findings of the IPS Prism Survey. Three speakers gave their own views on the future. With the change in the landscape of media and communications, civil society and active citizens are not just willing but also able to generate of their own social and political movements. This is no longer the preserve of the strong Singapore state or political parties. One speaker expressed his desire to see a more collaborative and synergistic relationship between the government and the people sector than what exists at the moment. The opposition political leader, Ms Sylvia Lim of the Workers' Party and Member of Parliament, Aljunied Group Representation Constituency said that there had indeed been instances of such collaboration between opposition parliamentarians and government agencies and urged that there be more. This collaboration should ultimately seek to improve the sense of well-being of citizens. The third speaker emphasised the real need for developing a sense of trust among citizens in the midst of all the other lofty aspirations we have for good governance — increased transparency of government, robust civic institutions and so on. The media and communications revolution must be accompanied by a higher level of critical analysis of information and other content for it to truly benefit governance. The growing diversity of Singapore society could mean that dominant values are contested, but there must be ways to ensure it strengthens the community, not weaken it. These discussions can be found in the third section of this book.

The conference closed with a landmark dialogue session with the Prime Minister of Singapore, Mr Lee Hsien Loong, who was candid in assessing the recent past of policy-making and political developments, and peripatetic in his comparative analysis of governance systems that were suggested for Singapore by members of the audience that day.

There was clearly a high level of passion and commitment demonstrated by speakers and participants at the conference for improving the way we govern ourselves as a country.

I would like to thank to all who contributed to the IPS Prism project, the speakers, participants at the Singapore Perspectives Conference 2013 for sharing their insights, the IPS administration team who ensured the smooth running of both the project and conference, as well as copy-editors, Ms Leong Wenshan and Ms Sandhya for their work on this book.

The Residual

CHAPTER 1

Governance in Singapore: History and Legacy

CHAN HENG CHEE

INTRODUCTION

History to a large extent explains why countries have particular political traditions, why they hold certain values dear and why they develop characteristic responses and reflexes. Over time, countries and people develop habits of the heart and of the mind.

There is the American political model with identifiable American values and reflexes, and even though administrations change and different parties take over, the American political model remains and the political reflexes are quite predictable. The Second Amendment to the American Constitution introduced in 1791 spells out the right to bear arms. Today, after so many cases of shootings in schools and a groundswell of anti-gun feelings, it is still difficult to take away that right. The gun lobby is strong and the current American President, Barack Obama and all those who want to do something about the senseless killings can only talk about outlawing specific types of guns and introducing more stringent checks, and even that is pushed back. Now President Obama is talking about using a presidential decree to push through a new law.

There is the Chinese Communist model. The Chinese Communist Party (CCP) underwent change with Deng Xiaoping's "Four Modernisations" — ideology weakened, some would say evaporated, but the Party remains strong. Many of the reflexes and traditions remain.

But change does occur and must occur as a country develops, and this is sometimes a rapid fundamental change. America had its counterculture revolution triggered by the Vietnam War. There were some major social value changes, especially with the women's movement and Black Power, where existing authority structures were profoundly challenged and questioned. There was significant social change, and even though there was change in the political culture too, the political and governing model remained more or less the same. The first African–American president was only elected in 2008. Change in political model seems to lag behind change in political culture.

I go into some length about the United States (US) because it is a country I have come to know, and I find it helpful to reflect on other countries when thinking about history and political change in Singapore.

Then, there are revolutions like the Arab Spring that can disrupt a model and overthrow institutions. Revolutions are often followed by a period of adjustment that is often long and difficult, but even then, some core values and reflexes can resurface.

"SINGAPORE EXCEPTIONALISM"

Every country claims exceptionalism. President Obama reminded Americans that when they think of themselves as an exceptional country and talk of "American exceptionalism" they should remember the French too claim exceptionalism, and there is "German exceptionalism", "South African exceptionalism", and so on.

I would like to speak of "Singapore exceptionalism", for in many ways we are an exceptional country. I say this not to be proud or arrogant, but to recognise that we are *sui generis* — unique, of its own kind. We are an unlikely nation, the only city-state that is also nation-state in the world. We are a micro-state and one that has developed to its furthest, the strategy of small state survival. We did not have to develop this way: a successful country with a record of enviable growth for more than four decades. It could have gone the other way. Americans tell me all the time that we are a small country that gets things done. When we say we will do something, we do it — for instance, how many times have we reformed the education system hoping each time to make it better? Foreign diplomats in Singapore marvel at the way Singapore and Singaporeans have a "can do" mentality.

Some frankly say that in their countries they spend so much time arguing about things that nothing or very little gets implemented in the end.

(An aside: I just read in an Economist Intelligence Unit or EIU global survey in which people were asked which country they would want to be born in, Singapore ranked number six. All the Nordic countries ranked near the top. EIU concluded that people wanted to be born in a country that is small, peaceful and homogeneous and a liberal democracy, but Singapore surprised them completely.[1])

Why is Singapore the way it is? What is the political model we have developed? What are our governing reflexes and national shared values? In Singapore, and after the 2011 General Election, there is a great deal of talk about the change needed. There are those who focus on the policy changes they would like to see. But there is a segment that wants to see change in the political model — into a Western-style democracy with a two-party system.

This chapter reflects on the Singapore situation: what we are, why we are what we are and where we will be heading.

SINGAPORE'S HISTORY AND LEGACY

I began by setting out how historical circumstances shape values, tradition and governing models. Let me quickly go through some historical facts to make a few points. In 1965, Singapore achieved independence unexpectedly. Survival was the issue, front and centre. Singaporeans could feel it. What would our future be? What next? We had no natural resources except for our people and our location. No oil, no minerals, no forests, no water and not much airspace. We had just lost our hinterland. We were not a normal country. Moreover, the immediate regional context was a hostile one. Separation from Malaysia was accompanied by explosive racial rhetoric and sentiments. Indonesia under Sukarno was pursuing *Konfrontasi* against Singapore and Malaysia, complete with commando landings. We were at our most vulnerable.

---

[1] See the Economic Intelligence Unit's 'The where-to-be-born index 2013'.

The Singapore government defined its first task as ensuring the territorial and economic survival of the country. The defence and foreign policy emphasised Singapore as a non-aligned country but accommodated the British bases because of the security context, and within a matter of two years, together with Indonesia, Malaysia, Thailand and the Philippines, we formed the Association of Southeast Asian Nations (ASEAN). So right from the start, we established Singapore as an independent, non-aligned country that is more pro-West and that believes in multilateralism and regional groupings as the way forward.

To build the economy, Prime Minister (PM) Lee Kuan Yew, cabinet ministers and civil servants went around the world securing foreign investments. They learned that political stability was the first condition foreign investors requested. In the 1950s and 1960s, Singapore went through a period of contentious politics of student riots, strikes and racial riots. Political debate was heated and passionate in the battle for merger, followed by volatile racial politics during this period. For our leaders of that generation, Lee Kuan Yew, Goh Keng Swee, S. Rajaratnam and Toh Chin Chye, of the People's Action Party (PAP), establishing political stability was the first order of the day. I recall PM Lee's words to the trade unions at that time, "don't kill the goose that lays the golden egg". Pragmatism was a lesson we learnt out of necessity. There was a sense of grave urgency, almost an emergency, to get the economy going.

The *Barisan Sosialis*, the largest opposition party, took the decision to boycott the first Parliamentary Elections of 1968 because they declared Singapore's independence was a "phony independence". It turned out to be a historical mistake. Once out, it was hard for the opposition to come back in. It was not till 1981 that J.B. Jeyaratnam won back a seat for the opposition in the Anson by-election. So without even working for it, the PAP got its first one-party parliament. They found it was quicker to implement policies and get necessary things done to respond quickly to emerging challenges to Singapore. And there were many. British withdrawal came earlier than expected, in 1971 rather than mid-1970s. This affected defence and jobs. There was a sense in the first-generation leaders that "life is tough, we are vulnerable, we don't have many options." The governing party played hard to maintain their one-party dominance, but they delivered on their performance. High growth was maintained, jobs were created, National Service was introduced, education expanded, and Singapore's home ownership policy was launched. Singaporeans gave the PAP government their support election after election.

The political model fostered was one that facilitated quick policy-making and implementation. It rested on a dominant one-party system, promoting consensus and an overall depoliticisation of issues. In my earlier writings, I described ours as an administrative state, an authoritarian government. But it was "soft authoritarianism" — soft compared to the Republic of Korea and Taiwan, which were hard military regimes. There was clear leadership from PM Lee Kuan Yew, aided by a strong bureaucracy with technocratic emphasis. Institutions were built to invite grassroots participation — Citizens' Consultative Committees, Town Councils, feedback sessions, etc. And there was criticism that the feedback flowed up but the policies did not change. Singapore's democracy is based on the Westminster model but is not an exact copy. Fareed Zakaria described Singapore as an "illiberal democracy". We have regular and free elections but not the freedoms he expects of a liberal democracy.[2] I have described Singapore as a "tight democracy". After the 2011 General Election and the by-elections, it is getting less tight and is moving towards a normal democracy.

From the beginning, PAP leaders enumerated specific values that were considered fundamental if we were to survive as a nation. These were, and still remain, respect for multi-racialism, multi-lingualism and multi-religions, which implies that seditious attacks on any race, language or religion will not be tolerated; maintenance of law and order; meritocracy; and non-corruption. Belief in meritocracy and respect for multi-racialism, multi-lingualism and multi-religions had a critical meaning in 1965. It differentiated us from Malaysia, from which we separated. They were two visions of a nation and Separation was about the contest of the two visions: equality of the races or preferential treatment for one ethnic group. Singaporeans have embraced these values, though now and again, there is criticism that the implementation falls short of the ideal. Singaporeans expect the government to deliver on these values. These have become our

---

[2] See Zakaria, F, "The Future of Freedom. *Illiberal Democracy at Home and Abroad*", New York: W. W. Norton & Company Inc, pp. 85–86.

national values. For sure, Singaporeans would not tolerate living in a disorderly and chaotic country where law and order is weak. There is a debate going on right now about meritocracy and its unintended consequences. Yet, I do not think you will get Singaporeans to agree on dropping that principle because any alternative would be worse. We debate to make implementation better. On the economic front, given our constraints in size and the small population base, Singapore had to be an open economy, linked to the world. We have no hinterland, and in 1972 S. Rajaratnam in a flash of brilliance said, "the world will be our hinterland". So we grasped the idea of being a global city in the 1970s before globalisation became a buzzword.

Over the years, the PAP leaders have modified their political style, but not the political model. It was a paradigm that worked. PM Goh Chok Tong's leadership style was more approachable and different from PM Lee Kuan Yew. PM Lee Hsien Loong has evolved his own style — part compassion, part firm leadership. With both leaders after Lee Kuan Yew, Singapore's political space opened up gradually. The success of the governing model and its policies is reflected in the positive changes in our population. So the ground has changed and expectations have changed.

The census data between 1970 and 2010 show Singapore's demographics have been reshaped. Singaporeans are better-educated, university-educated, overseas-educated and holding better jobs. The success of PAP policies over time was game-changing. Compare the education profile of the population in 1970, 2000 and 2010 in the tables below.

Table 1 Resident population aged 10 years and over, by highest qualification attained (%), 1970

Year	1970
No qualification	28.6
Primary	37.2
Secondary	29.8
Upper Secondary	2.7
Tertiary	1.3

Table 2 Resident non-student population aged 15 years and over, by highest qualification attained (%), 2000, 2010

Year	2000	2010
Total	100.0	100.0
Below Secondary	42.6	32.4
Secondary	24.6	18.9
Post-Secondary (Non-tertiary)	9.9	11.1
Diploma & Professional Qualification	11.1	14.8
University	11.7	22.8
Total Tertiary (Diploma, Professional Qualification or University)	22.8	37.6

Table 3 Working persons by occupation

	1970		2000		2010	
Occupation	Number	%	Number	%	Number	%
Total	650,892	100	1,482,579	100	1,898,042	100
Professional & Technical (1970)	56,080	8.6	-	-	-	-
Professionals (2000, 2010)	-	-	150,265	10.1	272,083	14.3
Associate Professionals and Technicians (2000, 2010)	-	-	283,361	19.1	434,850	22.9
Administrative & Managerial (1970)	15,476	2.4	-	-	-	-
Senior Officials and Managers (2000, 2010)	-	-	211,835	14.3	249,980	13.2
Total Classified as PMET	71,556	11	645,461	43.5	956,913	50.4
Others	579,336	89	837,118	56.5	941,129	49.6
Clerical	82,941	12.7	213,588	14.4	241,830	12.7
Sales (1970)	102,628	15.8	-	-	-	-
Services (1970)	88,744	13.6	-	-	-	-
Service & Sales Workers (2000, 2010)	-	-	182,966	12.3	252,606	13.3
Agricultural Workers & Fishermen	26,943	4.1	1,158	0.1	1,009	0.1

Table 3 (Continued)

	1970		2000		2010	
Occupation	Number	%	Number	%	Number	%
Total	650,892	100	1,482,579	100	1,898,042	100
Production & Related Workers (1970) Production Craftsmen & Related Workers (2000, 2010)	254,949	39.2	106,753	7.2	102,437	5.4
Plant & Machine Operators and Assemblers (2000, 2010)	-	-	178,752	12.1	151,579	8.0
Cleaners, Labourers & Related Workers (2000, 2010)	-	-	101,149	6.8	130,332	6.9
Not Classifiable	23,131	3.6	52,752	3.6	61,334	3.2

Sources for Tables 1, 2, 3: Census of Population, 1970, 1980, 2000, 2010 and Yearbook of Statistics 2012, Department of Statistics, Republic of Singapore.

The population with tertiary education in Singapore in 2010 was 37.6% and for those in the age group 25–34 years, 70.7% had acquired tertiary education meaning that they attained diplomas and professional qualifications or attended universities.

In 2000, of those at the university level, the proportion of those who studied at local universities and overseas ones was 48% (local) and 52% (overseas). In 2010, it was 52% local and 48% overseas.

POST 2011 GE

The general election of May 2011 was a watershed. A critical mass of voters sent a message to the governing party. They want a stronger opposition presence in parliament. The popular vote went 60.1% for the PAP and 39.9% for the opposition parties. More than one in four voters were in the 21–34 age group and about 8.5% of the electorate were first-time voters.[3] There were issues — rising cost of living, inflation, income inequality, and

---

[3] These figures are found in Chang, R, "Survey of young voters: Cost of living is top concern of GEN Y", *The Straits Times*, 16 April 2011.

the influx of foreigners that is perceived to be causing job displacement and the lowering of wages particularly within the PMET (Professionals, Managerial, Executive and Technicians) sector of the workforce.

The social media revolution gave voice to and amplified the dissatisfaction and opposition views. Singaporeans are now more vocal, more demanding of their rights and they want their views heard. They have lost their fear for speaking up and voting for the opposition. Politics has become competitive again. The political culture has transformed. Singaporeans have been repoliticised.

The ruling party responded swiftly. They were in a listening mode. They recognised the social contract had broken down and they would have to build a new consensus if they were to win back support to continue with its dominance. In introducing the public engagement process in mid-2012 called "Our Singapore Conversation", the government is seeking to provide an avenue for the broader public to express their political views and aspirations, and not just the politically active or social media savvy. The Conversation has shown that different people are asking for different things and sometimes they are contradictory. It has to be a negotiated consensus. PM Lee on 25 November 2012 clarified to PAP party activists:

> "We are not just asking people, 'what are your views and I will go and I will be your note-taker and speak on your behalf'. I think we have ideals, we have ideas, we have policies and we have proposals. And it is our responsibility to lead that discussion together with people in order to persuade people to see things more in the way we do."

I think the PAP knows it has to find a new balance. But it faces a classic dilemma: do you get rid of a model and a set of policies that have worked and in many ways continue to be relevant? The basic existential context of Singapore has not changed. The vulnerabilities are still there though they may be in a different form. Today the challenge is not about survival but about remaining competitive or risking irrelevance. And policies relating to our founding values of multi-racialism, multi-lingualism and multi-religions, law and order, non-corruption, meritocracy and open economy should not be given up for we will be diminished or destroyed. These are first-order governance principles. But other aspects of governance, what I consider second-order governing principles and policies, such as that of having certificates of entitlement (COEs) to manage car-ownership, foreign talent, housing prices, transport and policies that affect the cost of living should be reviewed and improved.

CONCLUSION

I read a very good nuanced piece by Jeremy Au, a young journalist at *The Straits Times* published on 12 January 2013.[4] He wrote about politics in 2030. Au argues that "if there is a consensus about the trajectory of Singapore politics, it is that there is an unstoppable drift towards liberalisation" and for some "the true mark of Singapore's arrival is the establishment of a two-party system." But Au points out that a recent poll in the National University of Singapore of 400 students "found no clear desire among the young for a two-party system."

How long the present model of a dominant party in government will last depends on what the PAP does in terms of policies, retaining its support and recruiting good political talent with political skills into the party. It also depends on how well the opposition parties do in recruiting talent and the policies and programmes they offer. We do not know what coming challenges in the external context could impose on our political environment, but one thing is clear — Singaporeans know what the PAP has done to build-up Singapore even in the past. They do not worry about sovereignty, territorial integrity or the economic future of the country. They take all that for granted. What the bulk of the voters ask of the governing party is "what have you done for me today?" Others simply support a bigger presence of the opposition in parliament as the kind of political arrangement they want to see. So going forward, the legacy is important, but it will be a competitive fight for support.

---

[4] Au, J, "Singapore Politics 2030", *The Straits Times*, 12 January 2013.

2

Three Scenarios for Singapore's Political Future

KISHORE MAHBUBANI

There is absolutely no doubt that Singapore is going through a political transition of some kind, but I want to add that most parts of the world are also undergoing some kind of political transition. The Arab Spring is an extreme example of that. We can even look at what is going on in the United States (US) and Europe as less extreme examples. The whole world is changing.

The middle class is exploding globally, and in Asia, it is estimated to stand at 500 million people. In 2020, just seven years from now, that Asian middle class is estimated to expand by three-and-a half times to 1.75 billion. What Singapore, Asia and the rest of the world are doing now is to try to deal with the rapid and massive rise of the middle class. It is important to understand this to explain the political developments that have taken place in this region as well. This also supports Professor (Prof.) Chan Heng Chee's view of the sociological trend that is driving political change in Singapore.

I agree with the broad thesis that: "the residual" does matter. Our history and our values *do* play a part in our political trajectory. One interesting point that Prof. Chan made in Chapter 1 is that Singapore's political system was previously described as "soft authoritarianism" but, after the 2011 General Election and after the recent 2013 Punggol East by-elections, we are now a "normal democracy".

You do not go straight from a soft authoritarian system to a normal democracy. It takes time. There is a transitional process. An interesting question that we should consider today is *how* this process began and *why* it began. The best way of understanding the power of the residual element in Singapore's political culture is to project it forward, to look ahead and see where the residual will take us. None of us can predict the future. There is an Arab proverb that says, "He who speaks about the future lies and even when he tells the truth". But at the same time, as emphasised by the Institute of Policy Studies' Prism project,[1] scenario planning does help. It helps to think about alternative futures. I thought the best way of trying to figure out how the residual will play out in the future is to think of three potential scenarios that might come Singapore's way.

The first scenario, which I think is the most probable, is the soft landing from soft authoritarianism. This is what you see happening in Singapore today. We remain peaceful and prosperous. But if we are to continue to do well, we need to embrace the fundamental values that the Singapore government has emphasised from the beginning. Prof. Chan lays them out in her chapter as the respect for multi-racialism, multi-lingualism and multi-religions, which implies seditious attacks on any race, language or religion would not be tolerated; maintenance of law and order; meritocracy, and non-corruption. We have more or less absorbed these fundamental values into our DNA, and so the likelihood is that Singapore will continue to do well. There might be more space for the political opposition and their share of parliamentary seats might increase, but by and large, the dominance of a single party will likely continue.

While I think this first scenario is the most probable, one of the most valuable lessons I learned from my first boss, then Foreign Minister S. Rajaratnam, is to always think the unthinkable. As we now know from the political transitions I cited at the start of this chapter, the unthinkable can happen. So let me address two other possible scenarios for Singapore.

---

[1] The IPS Prism project took place between June 2012 and January 2013 where the Singapore public were invited to discuss their views to the question "How will Singapore govern itself in 2022?" This resulted in scenarios called the IPS Prism Scenarios. For more information, visit the Institute's website: http://www.spp.nus.edu.sg/ips/ipsprism.aspx.

The second scenario is a hard landing. What is a hard landing? If you look all over Asia, there is a pattern of dominant parties staying in power for decades, then getting voted out, and then staging electoral comebacks several years later, like the Indian National Congress, the Liberal Democratic Party in Japan and the Kuomintang in Taiwan. The question now is: can it happen in Singapore too? It is important to ask ourselves what led to these kinds of changes, and how we can prevent them. These transitions generate much uncertainty and inherent risk, that can lead to a weakening of social cohesion and can disrupt economic activity. Incidentally, we should watch very carefully the outcome of the general and state elections that are due in Malaysia, this year. It is very clear that the ruling Barisan Nasional (BN) party knows that these are very important elections. I still believe that BN can win these elections but that seems far from certain. The mere possibility that BN could lose after 40 years in power is a sign of how political change is coming in a fundamental way.

The third scenario is also improbable, but we cannot rule it out because we see it happening in advanced democracies all over the world today. This scenario is political gridlock and paralysis. For example, the United Kingdom (UK) does have a government, but British friends have privately told me that they are horrified at the prospect of a 2017 UK referendum on whether to stay in the European Union as this means five years of enormous uncertainty among investors.[2] Even more strikingly, the world's oldest democracy, the US, as we all know, is also undergoing a remarkable paralysis. Recently, the Harvard economist Kenneth Rogoff published an essay that began:

> "Many foreign observers look at the US budget shenanigans with confusion and dismay, wondering how a country that seems to have it all can manage its fiscal affairs so chaotically. The root problem is not just a hugely elevated level of public debt, or a patently unsustainable trajectory for old age entitlements. It is an electorate deeply divided over the

---

[2] See speech by United Kingdom's Prime Minister, Mr David Cameron, 'EU Speech at Bloomberg', 23 January 2013.

direction of government, with differences compounded by changing demographics and sustained sluggish growth".[3]

If it can happen in the US, how can a small country like Singapore be immune to it?

This discussion is very timely. It is clear from recent events, including the opposition victory in the Punggol East by-election that we are going through a political transition here in Singapore just as the world is going through the same. It is our duty to try and analyse these trends as best we can and prepare for all kinds of futures and, as S. Rajaratnam would have said, to think the unthinkable.

---

[3] Kenneth Rogoff, "World is right to worry about US debt", *Financial Times*, (24 January 2013), http://www.ft.com/intl/cms/s/2/ed300802-63e5-11e2-84d8-00144feab49a.html#axzz2K0IU5luJ.

SECTION 2

The Dominant

3

Governing in the Future — Together

LAWRENCE WONG

INTRODUCTION

Over the past few months, I have attended many dialogue sessions and participated in many conversations. In these sessions, I have heard feedback and views on a wide range of policies such as education, healthcare, transport, housing, etc. However, beyond the policy issues, there is a search for something deeper — what Singapore stands for and what it means to be a Singaporean. One person I spoke to felt that Singapore had changed too quickly over the past few years, and that he no longer felt the same sense of connection with the country. Or as another person put it more vividly, "I would like to see a Singapore where buildings are not just commercial premises like shopping centres… I want Singapore to build and promote its traditions from 20 years ago, such as coffee shops (no air-con, please), *mama* shops, Malay barber shops, the old dragon design playgrounds…." So, nearly 50 years after gaining independence, Singapore and Singaporeans are examining "big questions" today: Who are we? What are our values?

These are critical questions as we try to make sense of the changes occurring around us. Life was tougher in the past, but fighting colonial, communist and communal threats, and overcoming deprivation gave older Singaporeans a powerful sense of shared memories and common destiny. There was a strong sense of group solidarity, loyalty to extended families and social cohesion. Today, our environment is becoming more interconnected, complex and uncertain. Advances in technology, the growth of global migration and trade have intensified the pace, intensity and volume of interaction between our people. All this means that the experience of being Singaporean has become more varied. Different Singaporeans will have different priorities: some needing to focus on meeting basic needs; others on wider aspirations; and many, a mix of both.

Ultimately, these issues of identity and social anchors relate back to how we want to govern ourselves. The roles of the government will have to evolve. Among our principles of governance are some enduring ones that continue to be important. After all, we have to deal with the same strategic realities: our geography, history and our multi-religious and multi-racial population have not changed. However, as new challenges arise, fresh principles will emerge, or we will need fresh interpretations of enduring principles.

In this changing environment, all Singaporeans, from the government and businesses, to civil society and individual citizens, must come together to forge a new compact that will allow Singapore to navigate the way forward. Governing in the future will mean casting new roles and relations between the government and citizens, and among citizens themselves, while strengthening and reinforcing values that Singaporeans cherish.

How should our governance principles evolve to address the challenges of the future? Let me share my views in four areas.

MERITOCRACY

First is the issue of meritocracy as a governing principle. This has been the topic of debate recently. I think if you ask most Singaporeans, they would agree that meritocracy has served us well over the years. As a small country, Singapore cannot compete in the world if we do not harness the talents of our people. Moreover, in a multi-ethnic society, any form of discrimination would easily have created resentment and tensions. So ability and performance are a fair and objective basis for making decisions whether it is appointments in the public and private sectors, or admission to our institutions of higher learning.

Having said that, there are concerns that with growing income inequalities, a system of meritocracy would favour those with means. This can undermine social mobility and lead to stratification in society. I understand the concerns. We all have hard-wired in us a deep moral belief and instinct for fairness and just deserts. We agree that people deserve rewards for ability and hard work. So when someone is held back by multiple layers of disadvantage through no fault of his or her own, it upsets our sense of fairness.

Clearly, when taken to extreme, unfettered meritocracy can lead to inequality and a winner-takes-all society. But that does not mean that meritocracy is inherently bad or dysfunctional. More importantly, if we are not going on merit, then how else are we going to determine a person's progression in school or work? I had a chat with several polytechnic students some months back, and they raised concerns about the stress arising from the national Primary School Leaving Examination (PSLE), and how this can be reduced. I asked them if they would prefer a system where progression to the next level was not based on PSLE, but on random balloting. No one wanted such a system. They all still favoured some form of academic assessment, preferably less stressful than the current PSLE, with progression based on merit. So we have to be careful not to throw the baby out with the bathwater.

The challenge for us is to improve our system of meritocracy. We do not want a meritocracy that breeds excessive competition, where people seek primarily to advance their individual interest at the expense of others. We do not want a meritocracy that results in a closed group of winners, where advantages to any individual are ascribed by birth. What we want is to shape a system of meritocracy in Singapore that works for the benefit of all and is consistent with our ideals for a fair and just society.

It is not going to be easy to do this, and there are no ready-made solutions. As Amartya Sen once said, the "idea of meritocracy may have many virtues, but clarity is not one of them." Policy-wise, there are things we can and are doing to keep our system open and mobile. That is why we have already initiated several significant changes in education, for example, by increasing state investments in pre-school so that children get an equal start in life. We will continue to study and review how our policies need to be updated to give full opportunities to every child, especially those who come from disadvantaged homes to fulfil their potential.

At the same time, those who have succeeded must think beyond themselves, and give back to society. They have to show that they care for their fellow citizens, for example, through philanthropy. We see this in the United States (US). People who have become rich are setting up foundations and doing good work. Mayor Michael Bloomberg of New York City was just in the news recently for donating more than US$1 billion to his alma mater Johns Hopkins University. Here too, many Singaporeans are donating generously to good causes. More people should do so according to their means and from their heart. Just as we embrace the value of meritocracy, we should also set new social norms for more giving and philanthropy in Singapore.

It is also important to have a broader and more appropriate concept of meritocracy — one that goes beyond academic success or achievements in a few selected careers. And we are in a better position to do this today than years back because our economy has become more sophisticated thereby creating many more avenues for talents in different areas to be recognised. We already see more and more young Singaporeans pursuing their interests in a diverse range of areas like the arts, fashion, music, sports, etc. We should continue to celebrate talent in these different fields and recognise those who excel, who overcome adversity, who show spirit, character and determination.

MARKETS AND GOVERNMENT

Besides meritocracy, public policy in Singapore has also been guided by a deep appreciation of the critical interdependence between markets and government.

The tension between markets and government is neither new nor unique to Singapore. It has been the central issue in the evolution of political economy and governance models over the last 200 years. The reality is that neither markets nor governments can work effectively on their own. Market principles are needed to help governments work better, and good government is necessary to help markets function more effectively. The balance between markets and government is never static, and has to be re-calibrated continually, according to circumstance and context.

The recent Global Financial Crisis (GFC) and the significant stresses associated with globalisation have put the spotlight on the imperfections and limitations of relying only on the market. I am reminded of what happened in my previous job at the Energy Market Authority (EMA). To manage the risk of our high reliance on imported piped gas from our neighbours, the government decided to import Liquefied Natural Gas

(LNG) to diversify our gas supply sources and enhance our energy security. A private company was appointed to build the LNG terminal, but when the GFC struck in 2007, project financing tightened up, and the project became commercially non-viable. We could have waited till the Crisis passed and allowed for some delays in the project, but we decided that this was important enough to our energy security that it could not be left to the vagaries of the market. So EMA took over the terminal project. We quickly set up a company, assembled a project team virtually from scratch, and with a loan from the Ministry of Finance, got the project started again. Since then, I have been keeping track of the progress of the terminal, and I am glad that in a few months' time, the LNG terminal will be completed, and we will soon be able to import LNG and begin our process of fuel diversification for energy security.

This is a story with a happy ending, of how the government successfully stepped in to address a market failure. And indeed, this is something the government since 1959 has done repeatedly in various sectors — from housing to banking, from the airline industry to military armament. But there are also problems with relying too much on the government.

Take again the example of our power sector, but go further back in time. Many years ago, the power plants and grid used to be owned and operated centrally by the Public Utilities Board (PUB). In government hands, PUB thought that they were doing all they could to be efficient and that they were ready for the functions to be spun off and privatised. But in private hands, the company (Singapore Power) realised that there were still areas for efficiency improvements and for costs to be trimmed. The privatisation and subsequent liberalisation of the electricity market brought more concrete benefits to consumers. Under the heat of market competition, power companies aggressively switched away from the more expensive oil-fired plants to the more cost-efficient natural gas plants. If the power plants had all remained in government hands, this switch to gas would probably have taken a much longer time to materialise and consumers would have been worse off.

So this is the challenge in public policy. The debate is not about nationalisation versus market competition as though they were mutually exclusive options. It is not about government intervening to supplant markets, or allowing market forces to reign unbridled with little or no government oversight. Rather, the real issue is about finding the right balance between markets and government, recognising that both are necessary.

The fact is that in our next phase of development, with slower growth and an ageing population, the state will have to do more and play a more significant role in funding or providing certain core services. The government will make significant investments in pre-school education. We are also doing a lot more to strengthen our social safety nets. In transport, we are making massive investments to expand the rail network and provide more buses. Another area is healthcare, where government spending will double to S$8 billion over the next five years.

As government spending increases, we must ensure that there are sufficient resources to fund and sustain the programmes we want. We can see the mistakes other countries have made — how easy it is for governments to spend beyond their means, and end up with large fiscal burdens and structural deficits. More importantly, state provisions have to be designed so as not to reduce the dignity of individuals, erode work ethic and create dependency on the state. Otherwise, after some time, the economy will stagnate, and the people will suffer.

So what we are striving for is not bigger government, but smarter and better government — one that understands the interdependencies between the state and markets; one that is responsive to the needs of our times, while maintaining the competitive spirit and drive that is so crucial to our existence.

ACTIVE CITIZENS AND STRONG COMMUNITY

The government will do its part to facilitate and lead in terms of the broad policy directions, but it has no monopoly of knowledge or ideas. To understand and tackle our challenges fully and vigorously, we need to draw on the expertise and resources of all our people. This leads me to my next point on the importance of active citizenry, strong communities and vibrant civic society.

Over the years, we have raised the level of engagement between the government and the people, opened up more space for civic groups and alternative views and matured as a society. The growing participation and diversity have been vital pluses for Singapore, enabling us to adapt to changing conditions and to the needs and expectations of a new generation. Going forward in our new environment, I have no doubt that our society will continue to open up. Younger Singaporeans, in particular, would like more space to express themselves, voice diverse views and experiment with new ways of doing things. These are positive trends; they show that Singaporeans care about issues and want to play a part in shaping the future of the country.

Governance must keep pace with these changes in our society. It means more engagement and consultation in policy formulation. It also means more effort on the part of everyone involved to listen to one another, to actively seek out viewpoints that challenge our own assumptions and beliefs, so that we can begin to understand where the people who disagree with us are coming from. Ultimately, we want to discuss issues with reason, passion and conviction; but always in a spirit of respect, so that people with legitimate but bridgeable differences can sit down at the same table and hash things out.

This is why we embarked on the "Our Singapore Conversation" (OSC) process. It is a process for the whole nation to have a conversation about what values are important to us, to engender a sense of rootedness, and to build a stronger consensus on the way forward for Singapore. Such engagement is not new — the government has been engaging Singaporeans in various forms and platforms over the years — but the scale and scope of the engagement are now much wider.

Besides more consultation and engagement on policy issues, we also want to promote active civic participation in solving problems. The late S. Rajaratnam described this as strengthening a democracy of deeds, and not just words. As he put it, we must "encourage participation at all levels to get people away from adversarial democracy to a problem-solving democracy." To facilitate this, the government should pull back from being all things to all citizens, and give Singaporeans the opportunity and space to organise themselves, and develop their own solutions.

Many have observed that when there is a problem, the first question people usually ask is: what will the government do about it? So at a recent OSC meeting, I was struck when a polytechnic student said, "Why must there always be a policy answer to all our problems? Why can't we solve the problems by ourselves?" Over the weekend, I had a conversation with university students, and the theme was "More than ourselves: A generation that cares". These young people reflect the coming of age of a new generation who are more active and engaged, and prepared to do their part for the community. We should encourage more of such civic activism to empower and support Singaporeans to take the initiative and make a difference to the lives of others. This is how we can nurture the *kampung* spirit in our urban city, and strengthen the sense of togetherness in our society.

LEADERSHIP

Finally, let me end on the role of leadership in governance. We have always believed that leadership is key; that as a small country, we need good leaders and able people to serve, whether in the political arena or in public administration.

In a new environment of active citizenry and civic participation, one may be tempted to think that leadership is no longer so important. On the contrary, I believe that leadership remains just as, if not more, critical. But the leadership demands are different. In a complex and rapidly changing environment, knowledge is always localised and fleeting. As a result, leaders are sometimes faced with an "inversion of expertise", where people at the lower levels have more accurate information, and are better able to adapt and respond to changing circumstances. A recent survey by the public relations firm Edelman shows that people tend to put more trust in their peer group, defined as a "person like me", than in traditional "authority" figures. Trust is being expressed in horizontal ways, rather than solely on a vertical axis. So the leadership approach must evolve to one that encourages more open collaboration, feedback and empowerment of our people.

We see this happening in the military. The former US Commander in Afghanistan General Stanley McChrystal once described how he had to adapt to a new leadership style, to operate in a complex, networked environment, and more importantly, to earn the trust and confidence of a younger generation of soldiers. He had to become "a lot more transparent, a lot more willing to listen, a lot more willing to be reverse-mentored from below." Over time, McChrystal said that he came to realise that "leaders aren't good because they are right; they are good because they are willing to learn and to trust."

It sounds easy to do all this, but in fact, leadership in this new environment will be more challenging. It means having the humility to admit that we do not always have all the answers. It means having the courage to take risks and to trust our people to make the right decisions.

With a more diverse population, leaders will have to gather a wide range of suggestions and ideas, and take time to build a consensus. It is not always possible to align everyone to the same view. So leaders also have to decide, explain the basis for the decisions they make, and take responsibility for the outcomes. As short-term populist interests gain increasing voice and traction, leaders must have the moral courage and integrity to retain the long-term perspective, and make the difficult decisions that will yield long-term benefits to Singapore and its citizens.

This ability to look beyond the short term has been crucial to the success of many of our policies. Today, it will be harder to take the long-term view, even as the government's policies and actions are being subjected to daily barracking. The daily incessant round of the 24-hour news cycle, its noise amplified by the social media, will make governance more difficult here as it has elsewhere. This calls for more, not less, leadership. And indeed this is not just a question of political leadership. It is, more fundamentally, about what sort of government we want, and the kind of society we want to be.

CONCLUSION

Meritocracy, the role of the state and markets, active citizenry, and leadership — I have touched on four aspects of governance where I believe our principles have to adapt and change in order to stay relevant in a new environment.

In charting the way forward, we no longer have the benefit of following and adapting best practices by others who are ahead of us. In many ways, we will have to break new ground ourselves and find fresh solutions that are suited to our circumstance and context. Increasingly we will have to experiment, make mistakes, learn from them, and improve ourselves.

More and more is now expected of governments. Some say that it is impossible to meet the high expectations. But almost 50 years ago, the cynics and critics said that a small, resource-scarce country with no hinterland had little chance of survival. In the 1960s and 1970s, some analysts thought in order to survive, a country had to be protectionist and favour domestic production. Singapore proved that we could be exceptional each time; we not only survived but thrived. We eschewed import substitution and found advantages from free trade. The "big questions" of today are the challenge of our generation. We can defy critics and cynics again if we answer these questions together.

CHAPTER 4

Sustaining Good Governance in an Era of Rapid and Disruptive Change

DONALD LOW

HOW IS OUR CONTEXT CHANGING?

The main issue that I want to address is how we can sustain good governance in an era of rapid and disruptive change. I believe that more so than before, Singapore will face greater volatility, uncertainty and complexity.

We have seen this economically: we experienced more shocks to our economy in the last 15 years than in the 30 years before that. Much of this is due to our growing connectedness with the global economy, to hyper-globalisation and unfettered capital flows, as well as rapid technological change that is shortening business cycles.

Politically, the government's space for manoeuvre has also narrowed. Its traditionally admired solutions in a number of areas — housing, healthcare, education, transport and infrastructure — have come under greater scrutiny and debate. This partly reflects a more contested political scene, but it also suggests that policy-making has become more complex, and the trade-offs, sharper and starker.

These economic and political trends will interact with social forces such as the ageing of our population, rising inequality, wage stagnation, lower social mobility and a larger foreign population to create new stressors on social cohesion.

Citizens' trust in the government's ability to deliver can no longer be assumed. The pristine "policy lab" in which our policy-makers used to operate is being replaced by a more critical public, and by a more diverse polity with competing interests. Increasingly, our policy-makers have to make *hard choices* — where there are winners and losers — not just remind themselves of hard truths in government. Citizens are directly impacted by the stark choices that the government makes, but their expectations of the government and the outcomes they seek may not always match what the latter can realistically deliver.

Sustaining good governance in this new, more complex and uncertain environment is not impossible, but it would require significant institutional and policy reforms on the part of the government.

THE RESILIENCE IMPERATIVE

In an era of rapid and disruptive change, the most valuable asset a government can have is resilience. Resilience is the capacity of a system to bounce back, not necessarily to its original form, but to one that allows the system to maintain its core purpose and integrity, and to continue performing its main functions.

Resilience — whether of an ecological system, an organisation, or a species — is usually a function of two things. First, a resilient system is one that has been exposed to a *variety* of shocks. Each of these shocks is not large enough to destroy the system but, over time, they force the system to adapt and to develop capabilities to respond to a wider range of shocks and stimuli. Conversely, systems that are fragile are those that have been insulated from external shocks or protected from competition. This is why the Galapagos Islands are ecologically so fragile, even if they are stable and seemingly sustainable.

We also saw in the Global Financial Crisis (GFC) of 2007–2009 how a lack of variety created a highly fragile financial system. The health of banks became tightly coupled to the availability of cheap credit, rising house prices and the willingness of home owners to continually re-finance their mortgages. Financial institutions mostly pursued a strategy of originating and then securitising sub-prime mortgages. The result was that there was too much mimicry and insufficient variety in the financial system. Such systems built on a monoculture can exhibit long periods of stability, but are also extremely vulnerable to the slightest shock. The collapse of Lehman Brothers had such far-reaching and catastrophic consequences, not because it was a particularly large investment bank, but because it was highly connected in the financial system in the United States (US). And because many other institutions were doing the same thing, there was a great deal of "interlocking fragility" such that when Lehman collapsed, the entire banking system became vulnerable too.

The second essential ingredient of a resilient system is *selection*. Resilient systems all have some mechanism for "choosing" between competing strategies and designs. We normally think of the selection process as being undertaken by individuals or leaders. Yet we can also think of selection that is constantly being undertaken by impersonal forces such as the market. Markets are resilient because they encourage variety and diversity, and because they are a highly effective way of selecting "fit" strategies or designs, and then replicating and scaling them up. As the economist William Baumol points out, markets are "innovation machines".

This resilience perspective, which I have used to describe both ecological and economic systems, can also be applied to the study of governance systems. If we agree that what governance needs most in the context of rapid and disruptive change is resilience, then we would also agree it needs to foster diversity and variety as well as competitive selection processes that are not reliant on a few individuals making the right calls.

While it is extremely tempting for the human mind to respond to more shocks with a desire for control, harmony and stability, the reality is that the avoidance of shocks and failures is a utopian dream. More problematically, insulation from competition and shocks breeds brittleness and fragility.

A political system can also suffer from too much mimicry and have too little variety to allow for the experimentation and adaptation that is needed for long-term survival. Without sufficient variety, a political system can become trapped by groupthink and ideological rigidity. The psychologist Irving Janis coined the term "groupthink" to explain poor decision-making by groups. Its key signs are a strong illusion of invulnerability by decision-makers, a belief in the inherent morality of the group, the stereotyping of those who do not agree with the group's perspective, and simplistic moral formulations that discourage deeper, rational analysis. Self-appointed guardians of the dominant ideology prevent alternative views from being aired and place significant pressure on dissenters, creating an illusion of unanimity, even if dissent is rampant below the surface.

I believe that this resilience perspective ought to replace the vulnerability narrative on which the government frequently relies. Rather than emphasise our vulnerability and how this imposes all sorts of constraints on what Singapore can do or can be, resilience thinking frames the discussion on governance expansively. It invites us to think about what institutional shock absorbers we need in a more volatile world, how we can achieve a better allocation of risks between the state and citizens, and how we should secure Singaporeans' confidence for the future.

BETTER INSTITUTIONS

Having identified resilience as the central imperative for our political system, let me suggest two areas of reforms that a resilience perspective in governance entails. The first is that we need better institutions, rules and norms to safeguard good governance in Singapore; the second is reforming meritocracy.

First, better institutions, rules and norms. For those who are familiar with the principles of governance that are taught in schools, there are four of such principles.[1] The first of these is "leadership is key". The elaboration of this principle is that given our inherent vulnerabilities, Singapore needs leaders of great ability and high integrity, individuals who will do "what is right, not what is popular." I think most Singaporeans will agree that effective and far-sighted leadership is essential for Singapore.

But if we apply a resilience lens, as opposed to just a vulnerability perspective, then we are likely to say that while leadership matters, good institutions matter too and possibly more so in the long run. This is partly because leadership is highly dependent on context. Good leaders in one context may make for terrible ones in another. Churchill was a great wartime prime minister, but he was far less effective in peacetime.

More importantly, the principle of "leadership is key" goes against the grain of the argument here that what determines resilience is not a wise man or a group of elites knowing the right answers. Rather, it is by ensuring

---

[1] The other three principles are: Reward for work, work for reward (or meritocracy); opportunities for all, a stake for everyone and anticipate change, stay relevant.

sufficient variety and diversity in the system that we increase resilience. In the long run, we are better off relying on system of distributed intelligence — on Singapore having a diversity of ideas and competing options, than on a system that is critically dependent on a small group of bright people.

So beyond the "leadership is key" principle, I would like to see a principle around the importance of having institutions that support dissent, variety, experimentation and selection. Translating this into practice would see the government give citizens and researchers more access to information, and support social science research as much as it does the hard sciences. Greater disclosure of information that is jealously guarded by public agencies and greater transparency of government's decision-making processes bolster trust in our system of governance and enhance government's credibility. Encouraging greater variety may also mean instituting the practice of red teams versus blue teams across government to encourage a healthy contest of ideas. Because the executive branch in the government has been a highly successful one, and one that has been relatively insulated from competition, the risks of insufficient variety and of inadequate pressures for it to adapt are quite real. It therefore has to make a special effort to create mechanisms that would foster greater variety and selection in the system.

Leaders of the governing People's Action Party have, in the recent past, expressed their concern about how increasing political polarisation might paralyse government. The greater worry should be about how the human desire for control, harmony and stability, might weaken the already weak incentives for policy-makers to allow competing ideas to surface, and to subject these to serious debate and analysis. In short, the risks of polarisation are less worrisome than the risks arising from the numbing effects of incumbency, the inertia of the status quo and the tyranny of old ideas for Singapore.

REFORMING MERITOCRACY

Second, meritocracy. This is a principle of governance that we hold dear, the practice of which should be tempered and reformed if we adopt a resilience perspective. The idea of meritocracy is that rewards should be allocated on the basis of a person's talents and abilities. But an equally critical question that we should ask is what *rules* should constrain the behaviour of those who have done well in the meritocratic system. There is no *prima facie* reason to believe that those who have succeeded in a meritocracy will channel their energies to improving society's well-being.

Indeed, as the GFC has shown, it is possible that those who have succeeded in a meritocracy may engage in morally hazardous activities and demand government bailouts when the risks they have taken go bad.

The kind of meritocracy that was practised on Wall Street also breeds a self-justifying, entitlement narrative. Wall Street bankers justified the decision to pay themselves millions in bonuses from bailout monies on the grounds that not doing so would cause talent to leave the financial industry. This kind of meritocracy breeds a belief among its beneficiaries that they are entitled to their rewards, that the market system is inherently just and that inequality is natural. They view those who have not succeeded in the system as slothful or lacking in merit and thus undeserving of state support. Such a system increases resistance by the rich to the redistributive policies needed to address inequality. Over time, it entrenches inequality and immobility, and society becomes more stratified and divided by class.

Singaporeans are often reminded of the risks and moral hazards of providing more help for the poor. This is the main justification as to why we must not have a welfare state. The GFC is a reminder that the risks of moral hazards are far greater when the rich are not properly regulated and reined in. Corporate malfeasance imposes much larger costs on society than the often-cited entitlement mentality of the poor who are addicted to government welfare.

So to conclude, I would very much like to see the principle of meritocracy augmented by a principle that emphasises fairness and social justice. Translating this into practice means avoiding conflicts of interest; ensuring the independence of public institutions; having strong safeguards against regulatory capture; and increasing transparency and public accountability. It also means strengthening our social safety nets and other redistributive institutions as well as ensuring a fairer allocation of risks between state and citizens, between rich and poor.

SECTION 3

The Emergent

CHAPTER 5

The Emergent in Governance in Singapore

GILLIAN KOH

The party that has governed Singapore since 1959, the People's Action Party (PAP), has had to face bruising political contests in the General Election of May 2011, where it suffered a 6.5% decline in its vote share vis-à-vis its political opposition. In two subsequent by-elections in May 2012 and January 2013, it lost to the candidates of the main opposition party, the Workers' Party.

These developments reflect a mood on the ground that people want change — change in the way the government relates to them and by which it designs its public policies; change in the way that citizens want life and society ordered. Also, diverse views about what those changes should be have emerged. Other chapters in this volume have addressed the different ways in which the model is beginning to change to respond to these trends. This chapter provides survey material to indicate what the ground expects. It ends by suggesting that the same political trend was witnessed in the other developmental states in East Asia, resulting in a higher level of political activism and expanding scope in social support by the state in them.

TREND-SPOTTING

There is, if we may borrow a term from the economists, a "secular trend" towards a greater level of political pluralism among Singaporeans. It is most likely the result of a growing sense of political competency as more Singaporeans are better educated and have become affluent, as referred to in Chapter 1 by Professor Chan Heng Chee. It is also reinforced by the transition of the younger generations of Singaporeans into the voting public, those who did not participate or witness the early battles of statehood. Products of a more secure society, they expect political parties to establish a connection with them, directly and in a way that respects their freedom of choice. They do not want their support to be taken for granted. Finally, with Singapore being an open, highly globalised city-state, the benefits of development have had a different impact on different people. While the state has made on-going efforts to redistribute the benefits of economic growth with more subsidies and social support, especially to the needy and low-income, these have been deemed inadequate, raising a sense of social injustice as the differences in incomes and lifestyles between those at the working class and the professional and entrepreneurial classes have widened. These are some of the social bases for the diversity in political interests and attitudes that have arisen.

Two surveys of attitudes about the general elections conducted by the Institute of Policy Studies provide support for the analysis above. The Post-Election Surveys of 2006 and 2011 indicated that the desire for political pluralism rose among the higher occupational classes, the more affluent and those who are better educated. The desire for political pluralism is also higher among the younger voters and possibly more so with each set of younger voters. The conclusions will be more robust with after we collect more data points, but for now the electoral results, the political discourse and these two sets of data can inform us about the changing relationship between citizens and the PAP, and their role in the governance system. Reported by Yahoo! News on 8 February 2013, a poll conducted by Blackbox Research of Punggol East voters after the by-election showed that while issues on cost of living were important to 39% of respondents, 17% said the government was not listening to them, of which one-fifth were below 40 years of age. Another 7% said they were guided by the need for stronger opposition to the PAP in parliament in their voting preference, and emphasised the role of a political opposition as integral to governance.

THE IPS PRISM PROJECT

In 2011, the Institute embarked on a year-long project called IPS Prism to better understand the trends in political attitudes among Singaporeans and seek out "the emergent" in governance, from the ground. The project was designed as a scenario planning process centred on the question: How will Singapore govern itself in 2022? Assuming two regular five-year parliamentary terms, the time horizon in the project would be two election cycles from the time the project was conducted. In the first of two stages of the study, 140 people closely associated with seven key sectors of society were asked to develop scenarios showing the possible trajectories that governance in Singapore might take from then till 2022. In the second stage, one set of scenarios from the first stage was presented with members of the public who were then invited to share their own thoughts about how Singapore would or should be governed. In this way, we were able to get a sense of what meanings people attached to governance; what concerned them and what their hopes were. This was collected in the IPS Prism Survey and constituted the third phase of the project. Its findings are discussed later in this chapter.

In the first stage, the top three trends that participants felt had the potential to shape governance significantly over the next decade, yet were the most uncertain in how they would play out exactly were first, the sense of trust and credibility that the government of the day enjoyed from the public — did they believe that the government served them and knew how best to serve them effectively? The second was how society defined success — by material standards or by non-material moral values. Third was how the social compact between government and people was designed — would it be one tailored to provide greater support to those with the most potential and rewards for the high achievers because of the benefits they bring to the rest of society, or a system that provided a more egalitarian system of distributing support and rewards?

Key concerns for the select group in this first stage of the project were the value system of Singaporean society, national identity and threats to social cohesion like income distribution, and trust in the government. In a democratic process, the participants voted on scenarios that they felt would be most plausible and yet challenging. There were 40 sets of scenarios that were developed in the first stage of the process. The set that received the highest votes in the final workshop, built on the three trends described above, were as follows:

SingaStore — a pro-business, high-growth world that the public trusts, which invests in people and endeavours that have the highest potential to create economic value. The question was how socially sustainable it would be.

SingaGives — a pro-Singaporean scenario where the public trusts a new government and elected president to implement an egalitarian policy framework that is supported through the use of the national reserves. The question was how fiscally sustainable it would be.

WikiCity — a pro-active scenario where a new coalition government is elected to trim the role of the state because of citizens' low trust in government, which allows for self-organising communities to emerge and meet the daily needs of the people. The question was how politically sustainable it would be.

These are the IPS Prism Scenarios.

THE IPS PRISM SURVEY

In the second stage, the IPS Prism Scenarios were brought to life in an immersive arts experience. Members of the public were invited to participate in creating exhibits and forum theatre designed around the trends and scenarios. They were brought through the IPS stories of governance in 2022, and then invited to share their own stories of "life in 2022". Using a method called "Narrative Capture" (developed by a company called Cognitive Edge), people who attended the immersive arts experience[1] or watched the material that was recorded and placed at an IPS Prism website were invited to volunteer their stories about what they thought their life would be like in 2022. They then answered a set of questions in what is called "tagging", which allowed researchers to find out more about the respondents' stories. There was a second set of questions that asked participants for their opinions on other issues related to their values and governance.

---

[1] The immersive arts experience was held at the National Library Building between 8 and 15 November 2012.

A total of 600 participants volunteered to complete the IPS Prism Survey. This was not designed as a representative sample of Singaporeans as it only surveyed people who attended the immersive arts experience or people who found out about it on the Internet. The profile of the respondents is as follows: 71.2% respondents were between the ages of 21 and 39, so they were primarily in the younger working ages; 81% lived in four-room, five-room and executive flats and private property, so the relatively affluent were over-represented in this sample; 81.2% were Chinese and 50% of them had no dependents; and 89% were citizens. This profile fits the younger, more affluent profile of voters who were likely to be inclined to support political pluralism, as shown in the earlier general election surveys.

What is good governance?

In the first set of findings, we pulled together views about the "goal of governance". When asked how they would judge the government, there was a bias towards assessing it by whether it "improves the well-being of people", with some saying that it depended also on whether it "delivers economic growth", or "'gives people the freedom to do what they want".

This result can be read from the diagram below, called "Triad 1". The dots indicate how respondents "signified" the story that they had submitted about "life in 2022" earlier in the survey. They were asked to place themselves in a way that indicated how they would judge the government in their story, or the sentiment behind their story.[2] Most of the responses were related in some way to governance that "improves the well-being of people". We clustered the responses by the patterns as indicated below.

The overall consensus is that attending to well-being rather than just achieving economic growth is what "good governance" should be about.

In another set of triads, respondents were asked for their opinions rather than to signify their stories. In "Opinion Triad 4", in relation to the "goal of governance", respondents were asked how they would like governance to be guided. The diagram "Opinion A4" shows that they were more likely to say

---

[2] Each dot in a triad diagram indicates where a respondent placed himself or herself to "signify" his or her story, or where he or she stands in the case of an "opinion triad".

that they want Singapore to be governed by "moral values" rather than "economic goals" and "common sense".

Triad 1: I would judge the government by whether it:

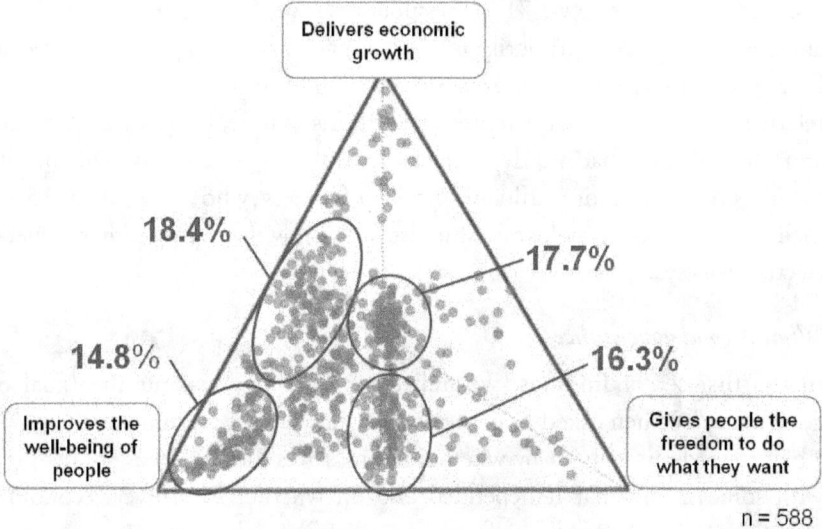

Opinion Triad A4:
In 2022, I would like Singapore to be governed by:

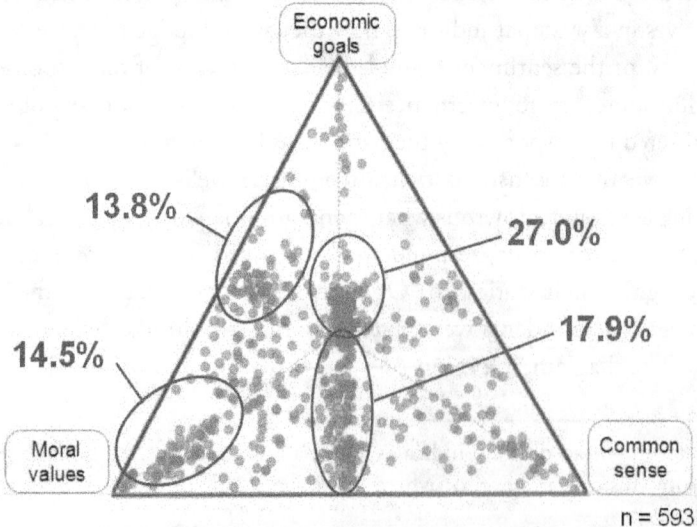

The result suggests that for this set of respondents, the performance legitimacy of the PAP government, that used to be based primarily on economic achievement, has run its course. Trust in government for this group would depend on its moral direction and ability to address the higher order goal of "well-being".

Who provides what and to whom?

The second set of findings has to do with who should provide basic goods like housing, healthcare, education and transportation, and to whom. As we find, in the diagram "Triad 2", the bias in responses was towards provision by the government with some role for the community. A quarter of the respondents, however, did indicate that these basic goods should be provided by the government, community as well as business sector. When asked which group should be given priority in receiving help from the government, respondents tended to think that it was the needy rather than "everyone equally" and certainly not "the people who can contribute the most to society". This can be seen in the diagram "Triad 3".

Triad 2: The main provider of what I need (healthcare, education, housing and transportation) should be:

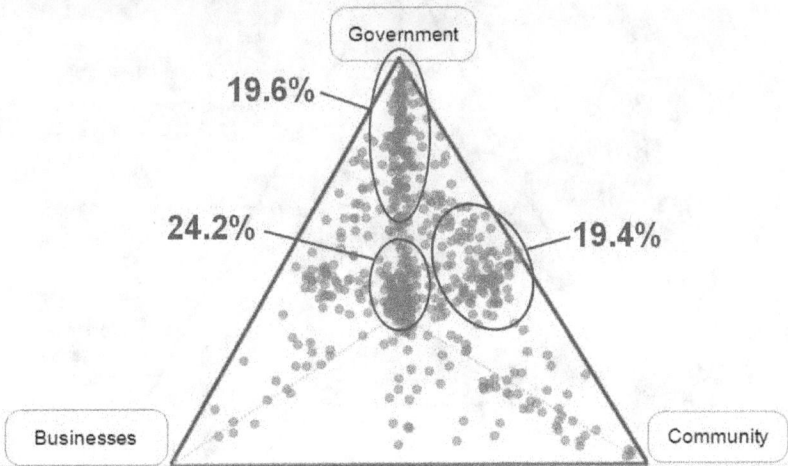

n = 583

Triad 3: The first to receive support from the government should be:

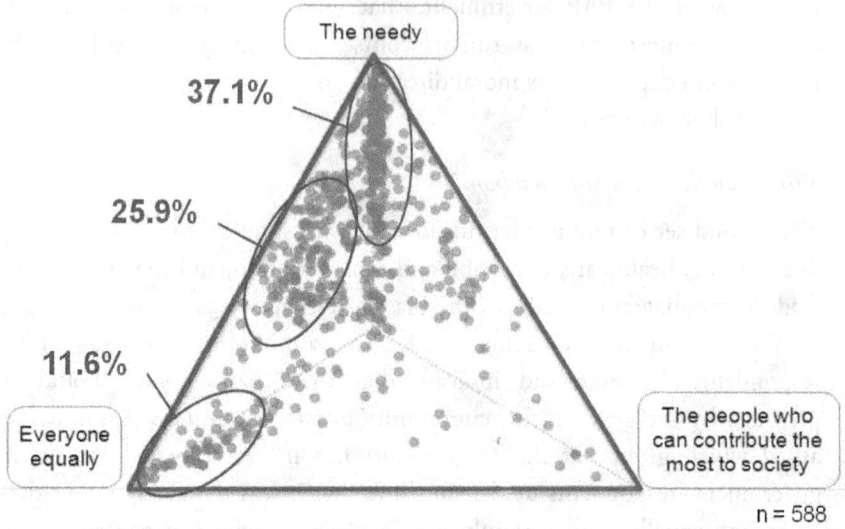

The needy

37.1%

25.9%

11.6%

Everyone equally

The people who can contribute the most to society

n = 588

Triad 4: The government should help these people first:

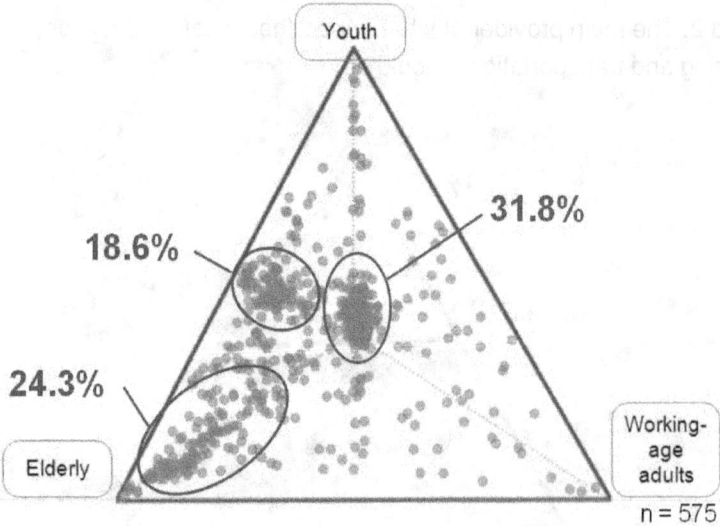

Youth

31.8%

18.6%

24.3%

Elderly

Working-age adults

n = 575

When they were asked which demographic group — the youth, the elderly and working-age adults — should be the first to receive help, respondents were more likely to be biased towards helping the elderly, as shown in the diagram "Triad 4". It should be noted that as many as 31.8% said that the help should go equally to all three groups.

What is the role of the government? How should it provide its support?

The third set of findings has to do with views on how the government should then do its part in meeting basic needs. As seen in the diagram "Triad 5", respondents were likely to say that the government should help people in a way that encourages independence and allows them to "help themselves", through partial subsidies of the costs of basic needs. Thus, for IPS Prism participants, big government would still be in fashion in 2022, and its support would be targeted specifically at the needy, the elderly, with the guiding principle of empowering citizens and subsidising basic costs of living. It is not, however, a typical form of egalitarianism where support is given to all as equally as possible.

Triad 5: The government should:

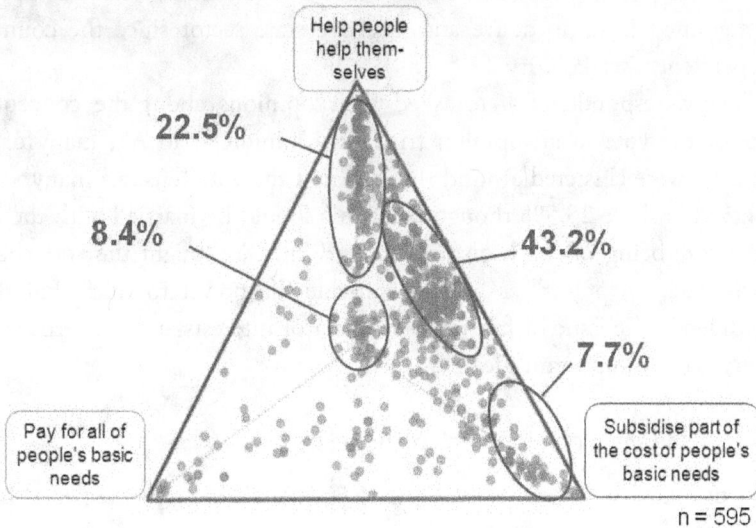

Help people help them-selves

22.5%

8.4%

43.2%

7.7%

Pay for all of people's basic needs

Subsidise part of the cost of people's basic needs

n = 595

Leadership and the Concept of the Vote

As a follow-up to the issues of governance, the survey also asked respondents to signify their story in terms of where and how "leadership" in Singapore would arise from and how it should be exercised. This time there were only two poles of opinions. In Polarity 1, the majority of the respondents felt that the government in 2022 was likely to "support new ideas regardless of the past", while a minority expressed that their notion of the government in 2022 would be "rooted in tradition, ignoring new ideas".

Polarity 1: In my story, the government

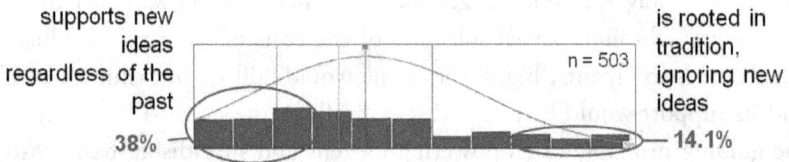

supports new ideas regardless of the past	n = 503	is rooted in tradition, ignoring new ideas
38%		14.1%

Also, a majority of the respondents were likely to say in their stories that leadership in 2022 should arise from the community or a mix of the community and government. This is certainly a shift from the situation where most would accept that Singapore has benefitted from leadership that has stemmed from an active and assertive state sector since the country's independence, see Polarity 2.

Finally, respondents were asked their opinions about the concept or value of the vote in an opinion triad. In Opinion Triad A3, many of the responses were clustered around the idea that the vote "ensures many voices are heard", where 25.5% thought that this should be married with the idea of the vote being "a check on power", and 24.2% thought the vote should "be a check on power" as well as "provide the power to rule". For these respondents, the issue of fair representation of interests and concerns across society was an important ideal.

Polarity 2: In my story, leadership should be:

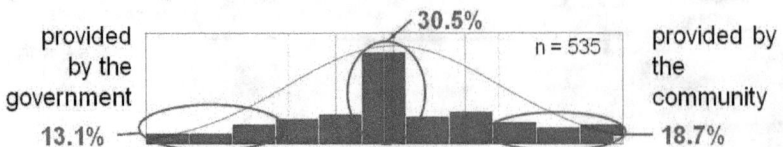

provided by the government	30.5% n = 535	provided by the community
13.1%		18.7%

Opinion Triad A3:
It's most important to me that my vote is used to:

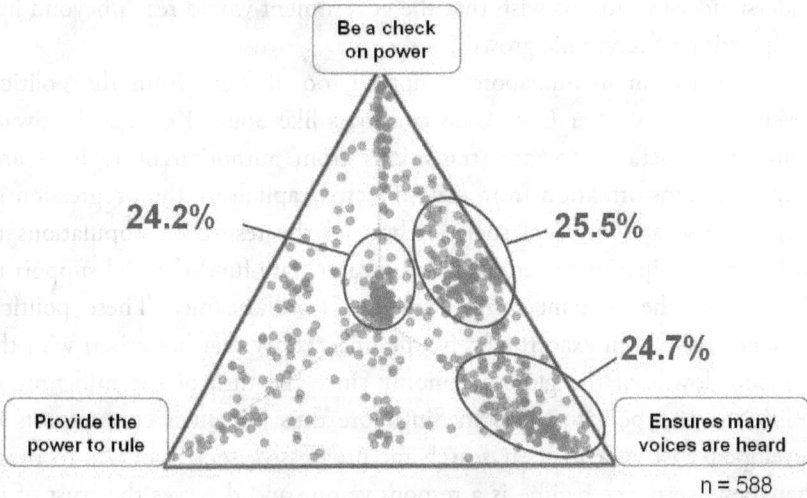

Be a check on power

24.2%

25.5%

24.7%

Provide the power to rule

Ensures many voices are heard

n = 588

CONCLUSION

Once again, while the findings do not reflect the opinions of all Singaporeans, given how the project is designed to look for "the emergent", an over-representation of the young seems appropriate to the task. While the expectation was that the state should provide for basic needs, with a great deal of consideration for the needs of the seniors given that we are an ageing society, the clear signal is that people of the IPS Prism Survey were post-material in their concern for well-being and liberal in their concern that the political system provides a good representation of interests across society. It is not the case that the material was unimportant, but that they aimed for the higher order goal of well-being.

They provide a context for the concerns about income distribution, the government's labour policy and economic strategy. There has been the worry that economic growth is being achieved by all-too-liberal strategy of allow foreign labour into the country. The argument is that wages are depressed at the bottom end of the labour market from large supply of foreign workers, and Singaporeans are crowded out from middle-management jobs (again from comparatively cheaper white collar foreign workers). There is also concern that Singaporeans are being crowded out culturally and that the city-state is congested with more people than its infrastructure can sustain. On this one policy point alone, it is possible to understand why citizens wish that the government would reach beyond just the question of economic growth.

The situation in Singapore is not all too different from the political developments in other East Asian countries like South Korea and Taiwan. Long after their democratic transitions from authoritarian regimes and economic transformation from state-directed capitalism, the progression to more diverse and unequal societies has led the respective populations to wish for participatory governance and greater state-funded social support to give people the assurance that their needs will be met. These political demands have been exacerbated by the uncertainty that has arisen with the ups and downs of the global economy since the turn of the millennium. Politicians and policy-makers in Singapore thus join their counterparts in developed East Asia in their search for progressive social policies to prove that the governance regime is a responsive one and deserves the trust of its people.

6

Civil Society in Singapore: Revisiting the Banyan Tree

NIZAM ISMAIL

"The Banyan Tree is pruned, and civil society grows and is embraced by the establishment."

This was an ideal scenario painted by an IPS Prism survey[1] respondent on Singapore's leadership and governance in 2022. It is interesting that George Yeo's seminal call — as Acting Minister of Information and the Arts in June 1991 — for greater civic participation by Singaporeans was revisited in 2012 and still seen as relevant.

Mr Yeo made that call for Singaporeans as citizens to be actively involved, not so much in the political arena, but in creating a "Singapore soul". This would create a deep emotional attachment to Singapore. His intention was to urge Singaporeans to enhance civic life in Singapore so that Singaporeans would treat the country as a home, rather than a hotel where people can come and go as they please with little sense of attachment to it.

---

[1] The Prism survey took place between June 2012 and January 2013 where the people of Singapore were invited to reflect on the different dimensions of governance and to work towards a future that they desire. The central question driving the process was: "How will Singapore govern itself in 2022?" Prism was organised by the Institute of Policy Studies. For more information, visit http://www.ips.sg/prism/.

The metaphor of the banyan tree was chosen because under a banyan tree, where the tree signifies the state, very little else can grow. When state institutions are too pervasive, civic institutions cannot thrive. Mr Yeo, therefore, argued that Singapore needed to prune the banyan tree so that civil society can thrive under the tree as some light reaches the undergrowth. He did say, however, that Singapore would always need a strong centre in the form of the government.

The issue today is the nature of the relationship between the state and civil society now — whether the equilibrium point in that relationship needs to be recalibrated.

This is the key issue that lies at the question of "Credibility of the Government", one of the three key driving forces identified in the IPS Prism Scenarios that will shape governance in Singapore for the next 10 years.

It is noteworthy that Mr Yeo's call for the pruning of the banyan tree was made in a very different Singapore. That was before the Internet became so pervasive, and well before the advent of social media and the Facebook generation. The political landscape was different.

Coming back to the banyan tree analogy, what we are really discussing is how much more pruning is needed so that the relationship between the state and civil society is a healthy one, or what sort of "tree" should replace the banyan tree, which represents governance, in order to strengthen the Singapore community.

Perhaps we could ask: is the government still uneasy about the role of civil society — cautiously tolerating it as a necessary evil at best, and treating it with suspicion at worst? What is certain is that today, we are far from the position where the state embraces civil society as a *necessary part* of governance.

I would argue that the banyan tree has in fact grown more dominant and domineering over the years.

In personal conversations I have had with political leaders, there is a lingering worry that civil society may pursue goals aligned with opposition political parties.

One such conversation related to the proposals contemplated or made at the 3rd National Convention of Muslim Professionals held in June 2012. The organisers of the convention, the Association of Muslim Professionals

(AMP), were told by political leaders that they could not pursue two particular strategies. The first strategy was a proposal to form a Singapore Forum on Civil Society (SingFor). This was meant to be a national platform where civil society groups could come together and discuss issues affecting Singapore. This strategy was not proposed at the convention because of the reservations expressed by senior political leaders before the convention was held.

The second strategy was related to a proposed formation of a Community Forum (ComFor). This was an enlargement of an existing platform — a Community-in-Review seminar held annually by AMP and the Centre for Research on Islamic and Muslim Affairs to discuss issues affecting the Malay-Muslim community. ComFor was meant to be a broader and deeper platform, largely to achieve similar goals as the existing Community-in-Review series. ComFor was also meant to track the implementation of the 18 strategies proposed at the 3rd National Convention. However, the ComFor proposal was rejected by political leaders who felt that an independent platform might threaten the existing state-sponsored Community Leadership Forum (CLF). This was despite political leaders having raised no objections to the ComFor proposal in earlier discussions.

The fates of the SingFor and ComFor proposals signify a continued distrust of civil society activities. In this respect, the branches of the banyan tree have grown to become more stifling.

Today's social media-savvy generation demands greater opportunities for civic participation. Social media has empowered Singapore citizens with alternative narratives and a quicker access to information, fostering democratisation.

The IPS Prism Survey responses support this proposition.

Part of the survey posed the following question: It is most important to me that my vote is used for the following options: (a) as a check on power; (b) to provide power to rule; and (c) to ensure many voices are heard. A total of 24% of survey respondents wanted a balance between all three options, while 25% wanted a balance between checking on power and ensuring many voices are heard. Around 24% wanted to "ensure many voices are heard". There is a clear preference by respondents to view the vote as a way to ensure that their views be represented, rather than to provide the government the mandate to rule.

Another question yielded a similar result. Respondents were asked whether they expected leadership to be provided by either the government or the community in their ideal view of governance in the year 2022. The survey results show a preference for leadership to be exercised by the community. Only 13% of survey respondents had chosen "government", 18% chose "community", while the balance of 30.5% wanted a balance between both the government and community. Interestingly, respondents from minority communities had a greater preference for "community".

What we can glean from these survey results is that Prism participants want to participate and take ownership of the governance process in the country. Bearing in mind that the respondents were primarily young, middle-class, single people, their influence on the political landscape can only increase. We can already discern a growing demand by Singaporeans to be actively involved in policy formulation. This must be seen as a positive development as it shows a greater commitment by Singaporeans to take ownership of issues that affect them.

Discussions by Singaporeans on social media are another important indicator of the pulse of Singaporeans. Regrettably, quite a few political leaders have characterised social media discussions as "noise". While discussions on social media do not represent the views of all Singaporeans, they do reflect the views of Singaporeans who take an active interest in issues affecting Singapore.

Instead of dismissing all social media discussions as "noise", the state should take a more discerning approach and *listen* to discussion threads on Singapore. If nothing else, do it because other Singaporeans actually pay attention to this online "noise", of course, some in a more discerning way than others.

So, there is a disconnect.

Political leaders are aware of the need to engage Singaporeans using social media. We have seen the proliferation of many Facebook pages of political leaders. The "Our Singapore Conversation" project uses social media for outreach purposes, and to get feedback. The ruling People's Action Party has also had an "Internet Brigade" since 2007 to present the Party's perspective and address online criticism on the Internet.

The broader disconnect is that there are already civil society groups in Singapore that the state can readily tap for views, but these are often dismissed.

The growth of civil society needs to be encouraged, not merely tolerated. Civil society participation is an important component of governance in Singapore.

The risk of not finding common ground between the state and citizens on where this equilibrium point in the relationship should be placed is that it will result in disenchantment among Singaporeans. The absence of platforms to articulate or address their interests will only frustrate them. If this were to continue, the "noises" on social media would inevitably take a more angry tone.

Beyond pruning the banyan tree of the state, I suggest that the analogy to the banyan tree be re-thought altogether. Rather than being a dominant banyan tree, the state could visualise itself as a set of trellis or an architectural plant support structure, allowing civil society to flourish within the state infrastructure, thriving as partners in governance.

And not as undergrowth.

7

The Role of Political Competition in Promoting Well-being

SYLVIA LIM

Last week, the Institute of Policy Studies forwarded me a copy of the report on the IPS Prism Survey for my information. One interesting finding I came across was how Singaporeans judge government performance. The survey respondents were asked to choose among three deliverables that the government could focus on — economic growth, giving citizens the freedom to do what they want, or improving the well-being of the people. Many of the respondents indicated that improving the well-being of the people should be the paramount task of the government.

This view that economic growth should not be the end game for governments is in line with trends in other countries. Economists have also written about the side effects of high growth — called the Paradox of High Growth — that tend to bring about higher inequalities and other social problems. There has been a moving away from Gross Domestic Product (GDP) measures as the key indicators of progress; in 2008, Nobel Laureate economist Joseph Stiglitz was asked by the French President Nicolas Sarkozy to come up with a better measure of social progress for France, while Bhutan's Gross National Happiness index is gaining traction internationally.

Sometimes this happiness index is misunderstood. It is not about emotions per se. Measures such as sustainable development, environmental conservation and good governance are key concepts. In July 2011, the UN General Assembly adopted a resolution entitled "Happiness towards a holistic approach to development" that was co-sponsored by 66 countries including Singapore. This resolution stated in its preamble that "the gross domestic product indicator, by nature, was not designed to and does not adequately reflect the happiness and well-being of people in a country." Member countries were then invited to "pursue the elaborations of additional measures that better capture the importance of the pursuit of happiness and well-being in development with a view to guiding their public policies." Since Singapore co-sponsored the resolution, we can assume the government accepts improving Singaporeans' well-being as a key goal. How does this affect policy-making? The devil is always in the details.

Life in Singapore has changed a lot over a short period of time, leaving many Singaporeans with a sense of insecurity and lack of a sense of place in the country. Urban renewal has wiped out most of our childhood memories. Singapore has also become a very unequal society. There was a recent study of world economies by Knight Frank and Citi Private Bank. According to their *Wealth Report 2012*, Singapore was listed as the world's most affluent country with a GDP per capita of about S$70,000 in 2010, beating Norway and the United States. It was stated that Singapore had the highest GDP per capita in 2010, and will likely remain at the top spot as far as 2050. This macro-statistic does not mean much on the ground, where people worry about healthcare costs, housing prices and competition from foreigners in the workplace. The need for stronger safety nets and protection looms large.

So what is the role of politicians and political parties in promoting well-being? The governing party's role is clear, since it is in the position of initiating policies and implementing them. But what about other parties such as the Workers' Party (WP)?

Our belief is that political competition is a safeguard to improve Singaporeans' lives. We provide competition at elections, requiring the government to convince voters that it is performing its role well. Outside of election time, it is also our responsibility to promote good governance.

In this light, having elected opposition members of parliament is important in several ways. First, we assist residents in direct dealings with government departments, and can see first-hand the effects and side effects of policies. Second, we run the local town councils, and can look in detail at the issues relating to town management which affect the quality of life of Singaporeans. On the other hand, the public also holds us accountable for our town management, which is a good thing as well. Third, we can keep the government accountable on matters of public interest by pressing for answers in Parliament, with the protection of Parliamentary privilege.

As political parties, we need to constantly check ourselves against getting too embroiled in partisan politics to miss the wood for the trees. The wood here is the people's well-being, which should always be the guiding light in our actions. We should guard against excessive one-upmanship and ask ourselves: where does the greater good lie? With this in mind, I have personally made it a point to make submissions to the government in certain policy areas that I am familiar with, ahead of any public debate. This is to enable the relevant ministry to consider my views fully and carefully. My experience shows that the ministries were objective and even took my views on board to revise proposed legislation.

Going forward, WP will continue to assist the government when we can and when it is appropriate. While political parties may fight electoral battles, I think it is possible to operate in a culture of mutual respect and give-and-take; it is possible for different political parties to co-exist in this ecosystem for the benefit of all and for the survival of Singapore.

8

Emergent Issues and Questions

LEE TZU YANG

First, I will address the work of the IPS Prism project that was focused on subject of this conference — governance, and then share some of my own thoughts on emergent issues and questions that arise when thinking about the future of governance in Singapore.

CAVEAT

My exposure over several years to "scenarios", used here as shorthand for the Scenario Planning Methodology, has made me more favourably inclined than many to their use. However, I am also aware of their limitations. Scenarios are logical and depend on an understanding or interpretation of connections — connections between the different factors that have an impact on a focal concern. In a complex environment where linkages are hidden, sometimes deliberately, and where reactions are sometimes irrational, we may have to look at other tools for strategic planning.

Nevertheless, scenarios serve to challenge orthodoxies, and are most useful in alerting us to possible alternatives to our current view of the future. We like to avoid thinking of possible futures that are unpleasant or contradict our beliefs. There is a need for techniques that help us to consider these futures, precisely because we wish to either avoid them or mitigate them, or adapt ourselves to successfully deal with these futures. Hence we should be careful in putting forward aspirational goals in our scenarios to ensure we have challenged our beliefs sufficiently and to effectively deal with uncertainty. Sports psychology uses visualisation to prepare the competitor to overcome the challenges to win. Aspirational goals serve as the incentive — to win in the case of sports — and scenarios stimulate recognition of the dilemmas to be overcome, and the effort required to do that. However events and trends are often beyond our control and the future often changes the "rules" with the participants playing a role in these changes. I will analyse each of the driving forces in the IPS Prism Scenarios to highlight the dilemmas that may have been obfuscated by the insertion of the aspirational goals about governance in Singapore, so that the full value of the exercise can be realised.

In the context of recent political developments within Singapore, the three driving forces that were raised and identified in IPS Prism as being critical to the question of how governance might evolve over the next decade, are largely internal to our society. A driving force is an uncertainty in the future that has great influence on the way we will deal with that future. We should be aware that *external* driving forces are often even more powerful. I will later introduce some of these external forces that I hope will enrich the discussion about governance in Singapore over the next decade.

FIRST DRIVING FORCE — CREDIBILITY OF GOVERNMENT

Credibility of government in performance and its motives was identified in IPS Prism Scenarios as the first key driving force. This is not simply arranged with believers at one end and doubters at the other. There are other dimensions to consider.

The motives and performance of government are perceived through a process of communication and debate on policies, the success of their implementation as well as the perceived behaviour of individual leaders. Singaporeans today do seek a significantly higher degree of debate on issues and results, and hold our leaders accountable to higher standards, both in transparency and behaviour. This is true of political leadership and also of leaders in other organisations in society, such as voluntary work organisations, charities and religious groups.

This trend towards more transparency and debate is not only a question of degree but also extends qualitatively to what is the rightful scope of government policies. The idea of "the common good" is subject to contestation, and it is different when referring to private and public domains.

If the credibility of government in general — not just a political party — is diminished, what will be the process by which the community makes decisions? How would the scope for such decisions be different from today? In what areas of life might they apply, and within what time frame? If the processes are uncertain as to how rules are agreed or decisions taken in the wider community, this will be reflected in the way people organise their activities, including in business where there are choices to be made like whether to invest in growth or to extend credit to other parties.

In such a situation, it will become even more important to look at the institutional framework for government. The rule of law, the independence of the judiciary, a competent and ethical civil service — all these and others provide the framework for the community to conduct necessary and important activities.

The strength and credibility of the institutions of government are important to ensure we are not solely dependent on politics to get things done. An aspect not sufficiently explored in the three IPS Prism Scenarios is the difference in credibility between politics and institutions of government, and how they might become more robust and independent of each other.

The issue of trust is not restricted to politics, or to the people and government. The big issues of trust today also impact business, through the expectations of customers, shareholders and the community in which we live and work, and from which we draw our employees. For example, there is distrust and a growing critique of the financial industry where societies have suffered from the Global Financial Crisis (GFC) from 2007–2009. This reinforces distrust of "big capitalism". How might Singapore society change in this respect, and how would this affect the links between government and business in the future?

SECOND DRIVING FORCE — VALUE SYSTEMS

The second driving force identified in the IPS Prism Scenarios was whether the dominant values in our society would define success in terms of economic and material rewards, or in terms of social themes such as justice, liberty and egalitarianism. This simple juxtaposition creates the tension needed in scenarios, but the situation at any point in time in society is of course more complex and is usually a composite of the above and many more themes. I think the real question is a wider one.

Unique personal situations will influence priorities, as will group pressure. Is a homogeneous society desirable for the purpose of alignment of values and nationhood?

To declare my own position on this, I believe in the value of diversity and renewal. I am convinced we would be a much poorer and less rewarding society if we all thought the same way. For instance, immigrants are important — not just as advocated for reasons of economy and size of labour force. The diversity of thinking, culture and values that immigrants bring will contribute to the development of our society. Conflicts may be encountered and "messy" situations may have to be resolved, but our society will become stronger.

With immigration as a feature of our social landscape, and with our own diverse backgrounds, we must expect dominant values to be contested. This is *not* a weakness and is necessary to bring together all communities. If we believe we must achieve a measure of consensus on what constitutes success, this must include some shared social values and satisfaction of material needs, and perhaps more. The way we treat those who have different needs, priorities and beliefs will distinguish us as a society. The way this diversity comes to be integrated under "one Singapore roof", which was not addressed in IPS Prism, will be one of the keys to our future.

THIRD DRIVING FORCE — DISTRIBUTION OF SOCIAL SUPPORT AND REWARDS

The third driving force identified in the IPS Prism Scenarios was how we decide the distribution of social support and rewards — whether policy should support "The Winners" or "The Rest". The argument for "The Winners" is that they create a multiplier effect to benefit the common good. The argument for "The Rest" is not only that this is the "right thing to do", but also because people are our only resource and developing the potential of all will ensure optimal development. There are clearly some links with the ideas of the second and first driving forces.

Again, the element of trust must be part of the argument if "Winners" are expected to bring benefits to "The Rest". This relates not only to government but to relationships among parts of the community. A complexity here is identity — with whom do we individually or collectively identify, "Winners" or "The Rest"? Is this dependent on the context of the question asked? Self-interest in the outcome, our own ego and our social and cultural values will influence our approach. And will objective measures in quantification, indices and segmentation be accepted, when they are never perfect?

Also, it is not possible to always pick future "Winners", not least because the context and criteria for "winning" is changing all the time. There is also a moral hazard in "Winners" picking "Winners". If we believe the future is going to be different from today, we need to allow more potential "Winners" to come through, some from behind, and others from places that we might never have imagined.

BEYOND IPS PRISM

My concern with the driving forces as identified in the IPS Prism Scenarios is not with how the electorate comes to agree with their elected representatives, but with how we come to agree amongst ourselves. There has hitherto been reliance on government intervention to help resolve matters. Going forward, the capability of our society to resolve issues without referring them to government will be a measure of our resilience and health. The issue of trust within society is paramount, and its importance will continue to grow if we seek the fruits of diversity.

As mentioned earlier, my other concern is that major externalities may come to have an impact on our aspirations for governance in 2022. When we do our scenario planning work, it is the externalities on which we need to keep an eye.

In the measures introduced to contain the GFC and turn around major economies, we already see efforts by the regulators to reach into and influence other markets and societies. Some regulatory developments appear likely to cross borders in our connected world. Singapore has been relatively insulated but this is not to say that we will always be so in the future. Our aspirations for governance may have to accommodate these pressures. External political developments may require re-assessment of whether our position today is tenable.

Finally, I am optimistic about technology although we should not be naïve. The impact on society of technology depends on the development of applications and the take-up in deployment. Technology will be as important as any of the other externality, but perhaps more so for Singapore given our relative affluence and openness. Technological change, especially that related to the Information Revolution will allow us to access information, observe and communicate with people and organisations in new ways that will shape our sense of trust and understanding of issues. Transparency of data will require a higher level of literacy in managing data and information technology to ensure we have a higher quality of debate based on critical analysis and understanding.

On balance, technology should be a positive influence. New avenues to share information will offer unprecedented opportunities to collaborate on innovations. And I believe there will be opportunities for new "Winners" to come through from our midst.

4

Dialogue Session with the Prime Minister

Dialogue Session with Guest-of-Honour, Prime Minister Lee Hsien Loong

Q: For close to 50 years now, the Singapore government has subjected itself to the electorate at sufficiently regular intervals to ensure its honesty in the short term, but it was also sufficiently assured of its position over the long term not to adopt opportunistic, populist measures just to win at the ballot box. Are you worried about how the government might find it increasingly difficult to adopt the long-term view, given how, as Professor (Prof.) Chan Heng Chee said earlier at this conference, Singapore is becoming a "normal democracy" now?

A: It is a challenge for us and governments all over the world, even strong ones. Mayor of New York City Mr Michael Bloomberg who was here last year to receive a prize, said how difficult governing was because the social media made governance a "24/7 referendum". Before the day was out, what he said in Singapore had been reported back in America and slammed in the social media. He had to back pedal, which ironically proved his point. I do not think we can be exempt from these pressures; any government will have to manage them. But if Singapore is going to prosper, it must be able to look beyond these pressures and take measures that make sense well beyond the next election.

Can it be done? It depends on the quality of leadership and whether leaders have the trust and confidence of the population. I think it also depends on whether the population is able to stand back and take a collective view of what is good for Singapore. It is our responsibility as a government to try and help Singapore society come to a consensus on issues. We must all have a stake in growth and progress, and feel that society is going in the right direction.

Q: You closed the hustings at the Punggol East by-election saying that the PAP is still committed to standing "on the side of the people". There has been a lot of discussion today about whether the government can conduct a comprehensive review of policy areas such as healthcare, transportation and the social support system. In these areas, how you can reinforce this idea that you are "standing on the side of the people"?

Also, a participant said earlier that when people say that there should be more help given to the needy, he was not very confident that they would also be willing to step up to the plate to take responsibility for that. I suppose it is not just the task of the government. So how much more do you think people are prepared to pay the price of a bigger role for the state as you review those areas of public policy?

A: I think we are in fact moving towards more social support and greater transfers for the low-income and elderly. It has been the trend over the last 10 years, and certainly since I became Prime Minister. I think it is a response to the way our economy is maturing, the way our society is ageing, and I see that continuing. Do we need a more fundamental review? Well, with the OSC (Our Singapore Conversation), we are headed in that direction. We hope we will have new ideas on what we need to do to achieve good objectives without running into common problems, which many good intentions have led to, all over the world.

The Europeans started off with good intentions and they are in a deep fiscal crisis; the Americans started off with very good intentions with (former President) Lyndon Johnson and the Great Society; it has not been an easy ride for them and it has not totally solved their problems. So I think we have to do more but we have to find the right mechanism to identify how to do it and how to involve people in this process. We want to do it in such a way that people do not feel that whenever they have a problem, the first question that is asked is "what's the government going to do about it?"

Actually, sometimes, the answer should be "what should the government do less of" rather than "what should the government do more of."

As to how we are going to fund this and whether we are willing to fund this, I think that is a very legitimate question. Scandinavian countries are willing to go much further than most other countries: their tax rates are very high, their transfers are very generous, and people generally accept that, although even Scandinavians sometimes migrate elsewhere in order to escape the taxes.

In Singapore, can we go that far? I do not think this generation is willing to do that and I doubt the future generation will be unless we change very substantially. Although we can go further than the situation at the present moment, we want to avoid thinking that more money is the solution. We can find the money but the solution is more fundamental. If you are in the low-income band, the solution is to upgrade your skills so that you have more skills and you can earn better wages. If you are among the seniors and worry about your future, part of the solution is to stay active in the society longer. If we are worried about broken families, the solution is to try and strengthen our families so that they stay together, rather than encourage them to split.

These are all problems that we will have to meet. For many years, we told ourselves we are doing fine and have avoided the problems that others face. That is partly because we did some things right, but it is also because at that stage of our development, our society was young, the economy was growing very rapidly, and we could cruise ahead in calm waters. We have now gone beyond that phase and we have to adapt.

Q: When you talked about the OSC at another event, you said that the government could not be a note-taker and just compile a list of demands. But you also said that the party has to win elections in order to deliver. Over the next two general election cycles, how do you see this "new normal" in politics evolving, and in those terms, how do you see the government reclaiming the ground that it has lost to the opposition?

A: As I alluded to it just now, how the "new normal" progresses depends on how our society develops. I think the more we are able to keep our society cohesive, the easier it will be for our politics to work. If a society is divided, our politics will reflect that. If a society is united, then you will have different views, but we hope they are along a spectrum and not polarised and extreme. All this depends on the underlying economic and social forces, but it also depends on the way that political leaders play their cards — whether they are responsible or go populist, rabble-rouse and lead us into trouble.

As the government, we have the responsibility not only to win elections, but to make sure the country is governed in the right way and will work beyond the next election. The way to make it work is to try and bring in people who are both committed and have the ability to contribute to Singapore. You need people who can identify and "click" with the ground. It is a visceral thing — "Do I like you? Can I connect with you?" But you also need people who have ideas and can get people to work together to make things happen. Those are the sorts of people we are looking for as individuals, but more so as members of a team in the party, so that we represent the full population effectively.

It is not so easy to do that because you are looking for people who are not just professionally successful but also those who represent different streams in our society. If I have the right mix of such people with the right motives, I can make it work. It is not certain, but that is the way to maximise our chances.

Q: With increasing political pluralism in Singapore, which is sometimes expressed in more adversarial or confrontational ways, to what extent do you worry that a future Singapore could find itself facing the same pitfalls as some of the traditional liberal democracies — plagued by divisiveness and stymied by the inability to govern effectively? If so, how can Singapore avoid these pitfalls, even as political pluralism continues to evolve?

A: These are risks in our system, as in any system. No system is foolproof. If you try to put a safety net to catch every possible mishap, you change the behaviour of the acrobat above the safety net. He does more ambitious, adventurous and dangerous things, and new problems will appear. There is no ideal solution that can help us avoid that. In the end, if you compare societies that work against the societies that do not work, it is not just the structure of the political system that makes a difference, but also the structure of society. Do the people in it feel at one? Is society stable? Are the people able to work out their differences, or do they become polarised and agitated?

Indian democracy works very differently from Swiss democracy, but the latter is not half as exciting as the former — you do not even know who the President is, because the ministers take turns to be the President! We are not Swiss, we are not Indian. We must find a formulation in-between that suits the temper of our people. The temper of the population is gradually changing over time because we are open, our people are influenced by the world, and when you have a disruptive change like social media, it changes behaviour and outcomes, and Facebook is not the last word in disruptive change.

Q: Would it be possible to have a Freedom of Information Act and an independent Elections Commission in the near future? If not, could you explain some of the reasons why?

A: On the Freedom of Information Act, I would not be in favour of it. The people who have done it have found that far from assuring freedom of information, it could lead to more opacity and avoidance of records. If you know that everything you write down is going to be made public, a lot of things are not going to be written down. And if you know that the meeting is minuted, you are going to have a tea or coffee break before the meeting.

If you talk to some of the leaders who have been instrumental in introducing a Freedom of Information Act, like the British — I think Tony Blair did it when he went into government, and he bitterly regrets it — it did not always lead to the good outcomes that they had hoped for.

Secondly, on the Elections Commission, different countries do it in different ways. It is only very few countries that have successfully depoliticised it. In America, it is done by Congress, and if you look at the way they carve out their constituencies, it is explicitly done to preserve the vote for specific members. You have very interesting shapes of congressional districts. Someone once wrote a paper on how you could use a computer to arrange it so that it is as neat as possible, so that you have a logical electorate to elect congressmen. It never happened.

So I do not think there is a good solution that can depoliticise the process. I think it is better to leave it as it is in Singapore — the Prime Minister appoints an electoral boundaries commission, it puts out the report, and you can see that it is on the whole, balanced and fair. If you look at the last general election, there were a few quibbles here and there, but by and large, people acknowledged it was a fair demarcation.

Q: Short of a Freedom of Information Act, could the government do more to release information than it is now doing?

A: I think that is possible, and in fact we have been doing that. I sometimes think we put out so much information that people are snowed under, and when they say, "you didn't tell us", what they mean is "we didn't hear you". I think we need to have better impact when we put the information out, and there will be records and things where — if they are not sensitive — we should be quite prepared to share. Nowadays, if you can put out the information, people can 'mash' it up and use it; they can do a lot of clever things with it, which can be helpful, and we are encouraging that.

Q: This morning, Prof. Chan Heng Chee and Prof. Kishore Mahbubani talked about political change and how Singapore is heading towards becoming a "more normal" democracy. They discussed several scenarios and proposed a "soft landing" from a soft authoritarian government as the best outcome. They identified four core fundamentals that characterised our government's overarching policies: a multi-racial, multi-lingual, multi-religious approach; maintenance of law and order; meritocracy; and a non-corrupt government. I understand these to be the non-negotiables in our governance system. Would you agree with this overarching model of governance?

Secondly, it was mooted that political expectations have changed significantly since GE 2011, and there is no turning back as our political DNA now evolves towards a more "normal democracy", with a better-educated and more sophisticated electorate. Will the PAP re-strategise to engage this new landscape? Would the PAP also look at the rules of engagement with the emerging opposition members of parliament (MPs)

for example in the issue of management of town councils, and as was suggested at the last session, perhaps introduce mayoral elections?

A: I think the four principles that Prof. Chan and Prof. Mahbubani described are in fact fundamental principles. They may not be the only ones — there are other issues any government will have to think about, not least being how to secure the livelihoods of Singaporeans, which is not to be taken for granted. But meritocracy, multi-racialism, incorruptibility, and law and order are basic; without them, the system goes down the drain.

I do not know what landing we will reach from the *status quo*. I think we started in an exceptional position after independence, with the PAP in an overwhelmingly dominant position. I think the PAP is still in a very strong position, but a generation from now, I am sure the landscape will have changed. I hope we can get from here to there in a stable, predictable and secure way. It is not to be taken for granted, but it is something we have to work towards.

I am not sure whether we want to have more levels of elections in Singapore. There are certain economies of scale, but you do not want it to become too multi-layered, because then it becomes very difficult and you spend all your time doing elections, which is what happens in Taiwan, for instance. One of our great advantages is that when people come to Singapore, they deal with the Singapore government, and that settles matters and you can proceed. You do not have to have a separate negotiation locally.

So I think we have to evolve. We have to find ways where you do not make decisions too centrally, but if you let the districts, mayors, town councils do more, we live with the untidiness. And you must be prepared to let people say, "Well I was in that town council and he was more generous to me, and why is it you are more strict with me?" We see that happening already. But that is the way it is. The short answer is: "If he's more generous to you, you should be there!" But sometimes it is not politic to say that.

Q: In 1933, then US President Franklin Delano Roosevelt introduced the New Deal to the American people, effectively creating social security and paving the way for many other US social safety nets. Today, as we relook our own social safety nets, may I just point out the trouble that having

wide-ranging social safety nets has gotten the American people into? Not only do they not have the financial reserves that we have, they are also spending themselves daily into larger and larger debt. While we focus on strengthening social safety nets, are we encouraging irresponsibility on the part of our citizens by guaranteeing them they will be caught if they fall off the line?

A: That is a risk, and a reason why we have avoided saying, "This is guaranteed. If you have no work, you can get money." Or "if you grow old, rich or poor, here is your entitlement", which is the case in many social welfare systems and leads to a lot of problems. You cannot say that you do nothing on the basis that anything you do will encourage people to become reliant either because sometimes, bad things happen to people, and we have to help. We have a mutual obligation to one another. The question is how we do it, how far we go, and how much responsibility we put on the person and his family.

Those of you who have been at meet-the-people sessions know that when people come to see you and you probe into their case history, very often you will find people who are in trouble, but they have family. If the family is poor and cannot help them, we understand and we have to do a bit more. Society steps in or we invite a voluntary welfare organisation to step in. But sometimes the family is there, and they simply cannot get on with each other. What do I do? Well, we try to help them, but it is not always possible to help every single one of them, and that is one of the issues we have.

One of the risks of being too generous with welfare is that it encourages families to split up. Then you have unstable families, and you have problems with their children in the next generation, which is what has happened with the Americans. But the present American problem is also a somewhat a different one. They have made reforms, tightened up and adjusted their welfare system, but the elephant in their room is healthcare, which is a big burden on the economy and the US government budget, but everybody is not prepared for the trade-off: they want to cut spending and lighten taxes, but nobody dares to cut, trim or rationalise Medicare, Medicaid or their prescription drugs scheme, which is worth hundreds of billions of dollars.

We are going to do more on healthcare because our people are ageing, and some of them need help to make sure that they can afford it, but we have to be careful not to end up in (the American) situation.

Q: We often speak of doing the right thing and doing things right. Could you shed some light on how government makes decisions and reacts to the public in terms of two distinctions — first, being populist and popular? Not being populist does not mean that we have to be unpopular.

The second distinction is about distrust. One could think about distrust as unhealthy, sceptical and non-factual distrust, but we could also think about distrust as positive concern regarding governance and transparency. How do you deal with these two distinctions so that, in reality and perception-wise, one will not be confused with the other?

A: Populist means you are doing something to please the crowd but is really harmful. Or at least that is how I would interpret it — it is harmful not to me but to the crowd. Popular means 'I'm giving it to you, you're happy, I'm happy'. It, maybe, does some good, and sometimes a lot of good. If I have a good housing policy and everybody has a home, I think that is popular. If I give the houses away for free, and I do not worry about how I am going to pay for it, that is being populist. If I talk about how I am going to spend the state finances without also setting out how I am going to raise the money, then I think I am being populist; but if I tell you that I am going to increase social spending and goods and services tax is going to go up x percent in so many years' time, I may or may not be popular, but I am doing the right thing.

I think what we are trying to do is to package our policies so that they can be popular, but beneficial to people at the same time. So when we are giving out Edusave scholarships or merit bursaries, or EAGLES character awards to students, is it popular? Yes, I think the children who come and get the scholarships are very happy they are recognised, their parents are happy. I think it is a plus. Is it populist? No, it is not. I think it is the right thing to do. So we make that distinction. If you ask another politician, particularly if he is not in government, he probably will have different definitions.

As for trust and distrust, I am not sure I would put it as distrust being a positive thing. I would say trust has to be nurtured. I appoint somebody, I trust him to do the work, but I also look forward to him keeping me onboard and onside, and explaining to me what he is doing, why he is doing it, whether it is necessary, what will come next, what dangers may befall us, and "to please have a care because tomorrow the storm is coming, so please prepare your umbrellas." I think there is a lot more need for that now than in the past because the population is more educated, a segment of the population is interested in what the government is doing, and specific interest groups will be very concerned. We are talking about green issues, social issues, education issues — each one has its constituency and I think those constituencies in civic society need to be nurtured and taken seriously. If we can engage them, that is a plus.

If we can engage a whole population, so that when we have a budget speech, everybody knows two-thirds of the measures that have been announced the day after, I think that is an outcome greatly to be desired even if it will take a long time to get there. That is because it is not the way the public works. Everyone has their concerns, their jobs and their preoccupations, whether it is family or career or some other personal issues, and they are not governing the country. So the government has to bear most of the burden but we also have to be open, and if we are asked about it, we will give you a full explanation. And sometimes, even if you do not ask, we will want you to hear it anyway.

Q: In the last general election, the PAP scored 60% of the share of popular vote but secured 93% of the seats in Parliament. That disparity between the popular vote share and the share of seats in the legislature is more than all the major electoral democracies in Asia. In that context, how concerned are you that Parliament may not really reflect the political complexion and aspirations of all Singaporeans?

With regard to recent policy mis-steps — namely the failure of housing and public transport stock to keep pace with an expanding population — how did the lack of co-ordination happen? Do you think Singapore would benefit from transparent and open discussion about how the mis-steps actually took place, in the manner of a public hearing or commission, to strengthen and improve the system?

A: On how representative Parliament is, I think there is a range of possible outcomes. Parliament is not meant to be strictly proportional to the popular vote. If it were, you would have a pure proportional representation (PR) system. The Israelis come close to that system and I think they have very unhappy outcomes because they are not able to have a strong governing party. If you have a first-past-the-post (FPTP) system, it tends towards a more decisive outcome and a clear majority for one party unless the electorate is highly split.

In Singapore, it tends to a more extreme outcome because we are so homogeneous across the country. In Britain, you have safe seats for Labour and the Tories. If you are in Cambridgeshire or the Home Counties, you are pretty sure that the Tories will win. If you are in Scotland, the Midlands or the working-class areas, the Tories have not got a chance. So you have two ends that are stable and you fight politics in the middle and the swing seats.

In Singapore, every seat is a swing seat. If there is a swing, it is a nationwide swing, and today it can be very lopsided one way, tomorrow it can be very lopsided another way. In fact, that is a factor in the very long term, for instability. In the shorter term, we have mitigated that by having a system of non-constituency members of parliament (NCMP) and nominated members of parliament (NMP), so while the People's Action Party (PAP) took 81 seats out of 87 after the last general election, nine more NMPs and two more NCMPs were added so today we have 81 parliamentarians who are from the PAP out of a full house of a 100. It is still heavy, but we have made an effort to bring in and have representation of alternative voices in Parliament. I accept that as we go forward, there will be more desire for a plurality of voices in Parliament, and I think that will happen.

As for the outcomes on housing and transport, we do not need to appoint a commission or an inquiry on them. I can tell you how it happened. It happened because we did not have 20/20 foresight. We went into the decade (2000–2001) starting with 9/11, the terror attacks on the US. The economy went into recession, our economic and population growth was slow. In fact, foreign workers went home in some numbers. House prices went down. We did not know how long this would last. By 2005–2006, the mood changed and the economy began to pick up. We decided that we should try to make up for lost time. You want Singapore to make progress, and you do not know how long the sun is going to shine.

As it turned out, the sun remained shining for longer than we expected. So the population grew faster than we expected, and our infrastructure did not keep up. Should we have given ourselves a bigger buffer and said, "Let's build and be ready"? I think in retrospect, clearly yes, we could have done more.

Could we have predicted that we would have five years where the economy would grow brilliantly and our population would increase so rapidly? You could not easily have said that.

Should we then have said, "I didn't plan for this infrastructure; let's tell the business to go away and let's forget about the growth; we don't need the IRs (integrated resorts); we don't need these extra jobs; we just stay where we are?" I think that would be very risky.

So we went ahead, and the strains showed up.

It is quite instructive how they showed up: not gradually, progressively, but quite suddenly. When the Global Financial Crisis came at the end of the decade in 2007 to 2009, we expected to be in for a very deep dive. In fact, in one quarter, we had almost minus 10% growth. Nobody talked about house prices, there was no shortage and the resale market was dead. But we did the right thing with our Jobs Credit Scheme and other measures. We dodged a bullet. The world economy recovered faster than expected.

In the middle of 2009, the wind changed. If you go back and look at the house price index by month, it was flat, but in June 2009, there was a tremendous blip, and in the course of two weeks, during one or two private property launches, somehow the wind changed. It was like the spring breeze touched your face, and the market was off! By August, we were thinking of measures to cool things down, and we have been trying to cool things down ever since.

So we lacked that 20/20 foresight. Next time we will try to do better, certainly to have a bigger buffer and not to cut things so fine, but I think it is very difficult to know 10 years from now, how much you will actually need. Even if you know how many persons there will be in Singapore, you cannot say for sure how many houses we will need. Will they buy or will they say, "No, I'm not certain because the economy is not looking good or because the politics are uncertain, I'll hold off"? But when the market goes up, it goes up with a vengeance, and we have paid a political price. We learn from it.

Q: In terms of the number of people — the immigrants — that you wanted to bring in, something which has become a big issue now, how did you decide what the numbers would be?

A: The immigrants are not really immigrants because many of them are foreign workers or professionals, and you do not know whether they will stay. From 2001–2003, when we had an economic slowdown, many of them went home, and their numbers dipped. Our attitude is: when things are good, we let them in, if we are a bit crowded, we live with the crowding; when things turn down, we let them go, and meanwhile we have benefited from them. We grew from 2005–2008 and shrank in 2009. But because we grew quite fast, in 2009 when we shrank, we shrank less than expected. It meant that fewer of the foreign workers went home than expected. That was a surprise.

Q: So on that point, how possible is it to fine-tune as you go along?

A: It is not possible. You have to take a stab at it, you have to make your best guess, build in some buffer, and even then, it may turn out differently than you had planned. If I ask you how many Singaporeans you think there will be in the year 2020, you can make a guess. Soon, we will be publishing the White Paper on Population, and it will make a guess of what that might be, and we will make sure we deliver a high quality of life for Singaporeans. If I ask you what it will be for 2030, I think the uncertainties will be even greater; so we can only make our best guess.

How quickly can things change? Sometimes within a few weeks, as I described to you when the property market turned in 2009, sometimes within a year or two. But to build the right number of houses and to build a train line or train network — you are talking about five years to ramp up the housing programme, 10 years to plan and build a train line — these are uncertainties that we have to live with in a very volatile world.

Q: **Earlier this morning, we talked about the need for building resilience in government. To build that resilience, rather than avoiding conflicts and shocks, we need to look at a variety of views. If we were to extend this argument to building resilience in our society in general, would you agree then that we need more space for discussions that could potentially be polarising or encourage a whole diversity of views? If so, how do we balance building a cohesive society alongside the ideal of having a resilient society?**

A: I think it depends on issues; it depends on the maturity of the population. For example, if you are talking about economic policy or social policy — should we have more welfare, should we have more state involvement, should we have more government ownership and nationalisation or more private sector involvement — these are things where a range of views are natural and that will be so in every country. You will debate them and the pendulum will swing — sometimes one way and sometimes the other. I think it is normal and healthy. It is a way to adjust to new situations and new political pressures.

There are other issues where discussions can easily and rapidly flame up. Race, language and religion are examples of these. You saw how Amy Cheong posted a rant on her blog and overnight, hundreds of thousands of people were very upset. Just 40–50 words on her blog! Race will always be a very sensitive matter; religion will always be a very sensitive matter. We discuss many things openly now where in the past we would have hesitated to do so: how our different religions shape our views, how our different races perform in school or how successful they are in society and in their careers, and these are things that previously we pretended were not issues. But to think that you can take your hands off and just leave it, is very unwise. Even in the arts scene, in a play, and even if you have something that is supposed to be a parody or a satire, not everybody will see the satire. And people can be grievously hurt, and understandably, look for some support or protection.

There are also other issues that are not related to race, language and religion, where we are not likely to come to a conclusion about them anytime soon. You look at the gay rights movements and pressures that exist in all the developed countries without exception. In America, they are much more open than we are, but the matter is not over because while homosexuality is perfectly legal, the next pressure is on gay marriage and full equal treatment. In France, there has been a push-back and there have been demonstrations in Paris against gay marriage. In Russia, where a lot of things go in many directions, there has been a pushback in the Duma, the legislation against gay propaganda or something to that effect. Conservative groups in the society do not want to see the whole landscape change.

So these are not issues that we can settle one way or the other, and it is really best for us just to leave them be, and well, we just agree to disagree. And I think that is the way Singapore will be for a long time to come.

Q: If I may go back to a previous question on parliamentary representation and push the envelope a little. On one end you have first-past-the-post, on the other end you have proportional representation, but there are systems that mix the two. For example, in Germany, you have a first-past-the-post system for constituencies; in addition to that, you have a slate that is distributed according to the percentage of votes political parties receive. Might that be considered some time down the line?

A: There are reasons why countries have done that. One of the reasons is because they need to bring in people who may not be certain of winning an election, but who they need on their team. Some of their ministers, for example, come in on the party slate, and then if you are high up on the slate, the chances are you will get elected and then you can form a Cabinet. If you do not have a party slate but enter on the first-past-the-post system, you do not have a safe seat and you may or may not get the minister you need. In an ordinary ministry, it may be less difficult to find someone to replace the incumbent. If you need a Finance Minister or a Defence Minister, it may not be so easy to find the person you need.

There is also one overriding reason why we did not go for a system that is based on proportional representation (PR) or even a mixed proportional representation in Singapore and that is because we believed that with PR, in a multi-racial society, you are going to encourage polarised race politics rather than centrist, multi-racial politics. In fact, that has happened. In New Zealand, for example, there is a New Zealand-first party, which is in fact a

Maori party. It could not exist except that they have a mixed-PR system. We think, and I think, that would not be good for Singapore.

Q: Prof. Chan Heng Chee mentioned long ago in a paper that the PAP and the government then was, or perhaps even now, is defined by its pragmatism. This morning, we talked about values, which you also raised: the four values of diversity, rule of law and so on. We have had debates about core values and national values, and one of them being the family for instance, which has not been brought up today — the building of block of society. Then we had that big debate on Confucian values and Asian values.

What drives you and gives your party and government a particular vision that enables you to deal with a whole slew of difficult questions now? Does our current system of meritocracy over-emphasise certain aspects of merit, causing the rewards to go to the "mandarins" and creating inequality along with undesirable jobs? Can we recognise non-academic merit and ensure that these people are rewarded for their contributions?

A: We did have a debate on shared values about 20 years ago, and we settled on a list including family, meritocracy, multi-racialism and a few others. At a broad level, I think we endorse them still. How exactly they get interpreted, what they mean in society varies over time, and different people in society will interpret them differently. This is why we never went beyond broad principles to elaborate an ideology, because it cannot be done. Once you put it down, what does it mean? Family as a building block — what does "family" mean? Family with one wife, family with two wives, an open family? There will be no end to arguments, so we just left it as a general principle.

What do we aim for today? I am not sure you can easily boil it down to one or two sentences, but I would say we are aiming for a society where everybody has a place, where we give everybody a fair chance and if you come from a disadvantaged background, I give you extra help to make sure you come to the same starting point.

Meritocracy does not mean money to the mandarins. I have never seen that interpretation before, and I do not think that is the right interpretation. Meritocracy means that I choose the right man for the most difficult job, I reward people for their contributions, but at the same time, I must also give everybody the chance to compete fairly in the race and I must make sure that the losers also get some consolation prizes.

How big a consolation prize and how you define winners and losers — that is something we have to discuss, and in fact we have defined winners and losers more broadly over the years because we want to recognise ability and contributions in many directions, not just with examinations or being a civil servant, but in the arts, social service, sports, and leadership. I think that is the right solution for us because we can mitigate meritocracy, we can help it to work better, and we can make sure there is always a hope that if you make the effort, you can take the next step up. You may have gone to 'N' levels, you can work hard, you can make it to 'O' levels, you can make it to the polytechnic, you can get to the university, and some people will want to do PhDs. Not everybody will want to do that, but the door is open.

What has made it more difficult to make that system work today is that the rewards have become stretched out, in Singapore as well as in other countries. If you are very successful as a professional, you can do very well financially — not just in Singapore but anywhere in the world because the doors are all open — and therefore the pressure for everybody to go up that single path becomes more than before. Within Singapore, we can mitigate that because we can say, "Well, you are a childcare teacher, I will make sure you are paid properly", "you are a schoolteacher, you may not be the top lawyer but I will make sure you are also paid properly", and try to balance the income distribution within Singapore and push against the stretching out, to a certain extent.

But it is not so easy to change peoples' mindsets. We try very hard to make sure that there are many other courses, schools, streams and options, but to persuade parents to accept that their sons or daughters can be happy in different ways, that is not just going to depend on what the government says, but is really going to be down to social attitudes and social perspectives, and something which we have to work at.

Q: The perception has taken place that the people who have made it in Singapore constitute a self-replicating elite. The word "elite" has almost

become a dirty word. In fact, this morning, Minister Lawrence Wong was relieved when somebody said he was "only almost elite". How do you deal with this? I mean, the fact is that although the PAP candidate in the Punggol East by-election (Dr Koh Poh Koon) came from a poor background and made good as a colorectal surgeon, he was nevertheless perceived as a member of the elite, and that the government as such, constituted by the elite, has difficulty establishing a connection with ordinary people.

A: It takes time, but if you have the right man, I am sure he can do it. I have no doubt that the candidate we fielded, Koh Poh Koon in Punggol East, would be able to connect to people face-to-face. But if you just look at his photograph and do not know him, then you do not know that, because it takes time. Unfortunately, we did not quite have enough time, and so he did not win in Punggol East. But I think this is a matter of social attitudes, a feeling that "if a person's succeeded, he did it through his merits, I would like to emulate him", as opposed to "he has done so well, why does he deserve to be there, let's pull him down".

This is a very fundamental difference between what America used to be and what Europe tended to be. I hesitate to generalise, but in America, it used to be that if you had done well like Bill Gates or Steve Jobs, everybody says, "Marvellous, I wish my son were like him and he deserves his billions". But in Europe, the attitudes are different. They believe "he must have exploited the system somehow. Cut the tall poppy down." We ought to have a system where people have a chance to go up and feel that "if my son is good, he can get there". I think that is not easy. Hong Kong has tended to shift from one to the other. Once upon a time in Hong Kong, people looked at the tycoons and said, "That's the way. One day I will be a tycoon too. Work hard and we will get there, like Li Ka Shing." But in recent years, they look at the tycoons and say, "I'll never get there, why is he doing so well?"

I think it is very important for us to keep the system open, that there is an elite — every society has an elite, you may call it that or not, but there is one. Even in a communist society, it makes a difference. In the old China of Mao, everybody wore a Mao jacket but the elite had an extra layer of wool inside to keep them warm in winter. So an elite exists in every society, but it has to be an open one, and they have to feel a responsibility to the society they belong to. Otherwise, people will ask, "Why am I supporting this system?"

Q: I would like to comment and appeal to you, as we bring in more foreign workers of the lower strata — highly skilled but not perhaps earning the megabucks — that we also ensure we have enough services and programmes for their well-being, and that our private sector takes on a more ethical approach in working with them. I think we are getting better and better over the years, but still, a number of issues have emerged that do not make us look good on the global map.

Regarding the place of social media, different political leaders seem to view it as a problem. Many of us will remain quiet in public, but when we go back, we write quite a lot, some of it is complimentary, some of it is not. Social media is a double-edged sword — sometimes it works very favourably for someone and sometimes not. I find that some of our political leaders struggle with how social media is being used, but it is part and parcel of being a public figure. Why do we need to moderate this when the community can moderate itself?

Regarding our older folks, even if one was 20 years old when Singapore became independent, today that person will be about 68. I note that a number of services for the elderly are not delivered with enough dignity. I wonder whether we could set up a committee or a review to look into how we administer the programmes — some of them are very good programmes — to our elderly?

Finally, I'm very glad that you put forward the issue on gay rights. I'm from MARUAH, a human rights group and I would like to hear your thoughts: with Singapore being a secular country, how do we reconcile that with an old and archaic law that discriminates against a group of people?

A: On foreign workers, I agree that we should treat them fairly, decently and honourably, and that we have to take a practical approach. They are here to do a job, they come from countries where life is tough, otherwise, they would not be doing this. They are here with us, and we have to treat them properly. But it has to be a practical approach and one that works.

Regarding social media, we do not believe that the community, especially online, will moderate itself. It does not happen anywhere in the world. Views can be extreme and people may respond in an extreme way. When people decide to disapprove of something that is inappropriate, the disapproval can also happen in an extreme way. It is the nature of the medium, the way the interaction works — and this is why we think it cannot be completely left to itself.

On seniors, you want their services to be delivered in a way that respects their dignity and I do not disagree. Please raise specific cases and examples and we can examine them.

On gay rights — why is the law on the books? Well, because it's always been there, and I think we will just leave it there. I have explained my position on this, we had a debate in Parliament on this [in 2007], and you can read my speech. It still reflects my view. As I also said earlier, if you look at other countries where they do not have that law on the books, the struggle does not end.

Q: You had mentioned earlier that all seats in Singapore are swing seats because we are a homogeneous society. However, does that not increase the risk of sharp shifts because of the Group Representation Constituency (GRC) system, especially with large GRCs of five to six member seats? Effectively, we have only about 25 constituencies in Singapore.

A: Well, I think every seat is a swing seat. GRCs mean you pool the risk in one and you decide as a group. The size of GRCs has come down in the last election. In the next election it will depend how the boundaries are drawn. I do not see the size of the GRCs going up, and I do not think abolishing GRCs is a solution to the swing seat problem.

Q: Do we have a roadmap to change our index of social progress beyond Gross Domestic Product (GDP), to include a basket of indicators such as well-being, sustainability, diversity at the national level and diversity in national decision-making? If we do, should the Cabinet Ministers' performance indices perhaps be based on these indicators as well?

You cited the incident of Amy Cheong, and before that you mentioned the principles of multi-racialism and multi-lingualism. There was much

criticism of Amy Cheong when she made the statement; in fact, it was addressed immediately. She made it in the morning, and by the afternoon it was already addressed. However, a former Prime Minister, who is also presently a member of parliament, was seemingly allowed to get away with the words "I stand corrected" over a similar issue. Should these words be accepted as an apology?

A: Firstly, the ministers' bonus is not dependent only on our GDP. We had a committee make a recommendation. Now, we have the real GDP growth rate as one element, the unemployment rate as another, low income workers' salaries as a third, so there are three or four things in what is called the National Bonus element of ministers' remuneration package. You can broaden the index, but I think beyond a point, it really makes no difference. The minister is not working because he will get 0.02% more as a special bonus at the end of the year. If that motivates him, he should not be a minister. The government publishes a report card every year on how we do in different areas: social services, economic growth, integration, education. So there is already a multi-dimensional index.

I do not think Amy Cheong is in any way comparable to what Mr Lee Kuan Yew wrote in *Hard Truths*. I notice you did not mention him or the book. I think he expressed a view, it caused unhappiness, and people took exception to it. He clarified his position and took it back. I think that is all he needs to do. It is another illustration of how sensitive things are in Singapore, because even to say that things are sensitive is, in itself, sensitive.

Q: Two questions from the Punggol East by-election. First, PAP is a party of renewal and succession. Will you prepare the next generation of leaders to be ones that are not simply super-technocrats but also people with good political and ground skills?

Second, you pointed out the case of Hong Kong on the perception there of frustration towards the super rich — I am a student of contemporary Chinese societies — that is indeed the case. Do you find that our lower-middle class Singaporeans are also feeling the same frustration as you mentioned just now?

A: On renewal and succession, yes indeed, we are looking for people who come in with technocratic ability as well as with ground feel and political skills. You need both. You may not find all aspects in one individual, but you need all of those skills in a team. That is what we are looking for.

One of the concerns with the way politics develops in Singapore is whether we encourage good men who have these skills to come in, or whether they shy away and say, "This is too nasty and dirty, let someone else do the work. I don't want to get involved in politics." Or even to say that "politics is a dirty business and therefore I stay in my profession or overseas." I think that would be a very bad outcome for Singapore, and it is very easy for us to get there without intending to, because you can sharpen arguments on social media, make it painful for the family, and good men say "why should I be there?" In America, it's a big problem — people do not want to be in public service because they want to avoid this very unpleasant experience and the country is poorer for it. We should try very hard to avoid that.

As for the lower middle-class in Singapore and how they feel, I think that this is something that we pay attention to. We are concerned that whatever your family background, you ought to have a full chance of doing well in school, in life, and in whatever your chosen pursuit is. It is very important that we keep on doing that otherwise, after a while, people will say "well, the rules are open but the outcome I do not accept", and then you have a problem.

Q: This question is dear to the heart of our ambassador, Prof. Tommy Koh. It is about a gracious society. You have used the term NIMBY (Not In My Backyard), and earlier on in today's discussion, two speakers mentioned that Singaporeans are becoming more competitive — not to the stage of dog-eat-dog but it tends to push out kindness and compassion.

An example: we were reaching out to the community and facilitating some discussions with the grassroots leaders in Yuhua and Jurong, and the grassroots leaders shared with us that when they surveyed the community on whether they would allow an old-age facility in their backyard, 90% immediately said 'no'. However, when they changed the question to ask "If your neighbour or neighbour's relative needed such help, would you agree to such a facility?" the response became 90% positive. We need to find a way to get people to change their mindset and see that such facilities are essential.

How do we deal with this NIMBY mindset? Perhaps this is one of the situations that you have mentioned where government can do less and let civil society take up the challenge of changing this mindset in our society; convince people so that this is not a top-down government-led initiative, and help them understand why these facilities are needed, consider the needs of others and perhaps become a gracious and compassionate society.

A: Your question is an example of my earlier point, where the first issue raised is "what is the government going to do about this problem?" It is a problem. It is a matter of social attitudes, of neighbourhood cohesion and engagement. If you are friends with people in your neighbourhood, you behave less as atomistic individuals and there is a sense of community responsibility. It can be any group, but we are in this together, we help one another. I think that is where you need social groups, civic society groups and non-government engagement in order to bring people in to network together.

There is an American scholar, Robert Putnam, who wrote a book called *Bowling Alone*. The point he made was that in the old days, Americans went bowling with friends, and therefore they had social networks, which helped them to be happier, live longer and do better as communities. Then the social conditions changed, families narrowed down, they went bowling alone, they lost their social networks, and that has weakened their society and made it more difficult for them to reach consensus. I think we are not so extreme, but we do need to form these networks in order that we can work together as Singapore and be a resilient society, and I think we will be a happier society.

Q: If you remember, about 10–11 years ago, there was an incident about a parent who insisted on his child wearing the *tudung* (headscarf) to school, and was told that this could not be allowed. Back then, at a similar kind of event called the Singapore Seminar, I made the point that Singapore is perhaps not yet a mature enough society to see past physical displays of religion like the *tudung* or any religious symbol that one might normally wear.

Fast forward to today and we have the Amy Cheong incident, we had the other incident of this person labelling a busload of *madrasah* students as future terrorists in his Facebook post. It does not seem to me that we have made that much progress in terms of multi-racial, multi-ethnic mutual respect. What, in your view, would it take for us to get there? Is it something that has to come from the government, or something that people must just one day wake up to and realise?

A: It is a very difficult question to answer fully and honestly. Religion is a very deeply-felt matter at the core of many of us. We have different faiths. It is a very important basis on which people identify who their closest friends, confidants and community are. You are Singaporean, you are Chinese, you may be Christian or Buddhist; you are Malay, you are Muslim. Each of these is one aspect of your identity, and for many Singaporeans, religion is a very important aspect of our identity.

That is what makes it difficult for us to say "it's okay to have any gesture of religious identification and it makes no difference." If we were just backing football clubs, you wear a Manchester United t-shirt and I wear a Tottenham Hotspurs t-shirt, you'll probably beat me at football, but I can live with that. Or you can wear a badge and I wear a different badge, and we can joke with one another. But if you go to school and you wear a crucifix and I wear a *tudung*, that connotes a very fundamental distinction. You may say that "it's external, it's unimportant", but these small symbols can cause people to feel less comfortable with one another, to cluster separately, and to integrate less, especially at impressionable ages in schools.

You have seen this happen in schools. We know this can happen in Singapore, and we watch other countries grappling with the same problem — some going for very draconian solutions. The French, for example, have made a rule that you are not allowed to wear a *tudung* in schools, and you are not allowed to have a *burqa* (a full body garment worn by some Muslim women) in public. Are we confident that we are well beyond the French positions? I'm not sure. I think over the last decade, we have made progress; today's position is not the same as 10 years ago. But at the same time, religion is a very important aspect of life of many Singaporeans, and more so today than 30 or 40 years ago. So we have to manage religion very carefully, and there are certain compromises we must make for it to work in Singapore.

. . . . .

About the Contributors

(At January 2013)

CHAN Heng Chee is Ambassador-at-Large at the Ministry of Foreign Affairs, Singapore and Chairman of the Lee Kuan Yew Centre for Innovative Cities in the Singapore University of Technology and Design (SUTD). She was appointed a Member of the Presidential Council for Minority Rights in July 2012. Ambassador Chan has served as Singapore's Ambassador to the United States, Singapore's Permanent Representative to the United Nations, High Commissioner to Canada and Ambassador to Mexico. Previously, she was Executive Director of the Singapore International Foundation and Director of the Institute of Southeast Asian Studies. She was the founding Director of the Institute of Policy Studies.

Janadas DEVAN is Director of the Institute of Policy Studies. He was educated at the National University of Singapore and Cornell University in the United States. Mr Devan taught English in various institutions in Singapore and the United States, and later wrote for various publications in the region, before joining *The Straits Times* in 1997. He served as the paper's leader writer for many years, writing unsigned editorials on a wide variety of subjects; wrote a weekly column on politics and economics, in which he covered international and domestic developments; and a column on language for *The Sunday Times*. In 2008, he became the editor of the paper's opinion pages, and in 2010, became the paper's Associate Editor. He also did a weekly radio broadcast, "Call from America", for Radio Singapore International, from 2000 to 2008, on American life and society. He left *The Straits Times* in July 2012 on being appointed the Chief of Government

Communications at the Ministry of Communications and Information. Mr Devan received the Clark Distinguished Teaching Award from Cornell University in 1988.

Gillian KOH is Senior Research Fellow at the Institute of Policy Studies. She heads the Institute's Politics and Governance research cluster. She was the project leader of IPS Prism, a public scenario planning project on governance in Singapore in 2022. Her on-going research interests are in the areas of state–society relations, the development of civil society, electoral politics in Singapore and the political attitudes of Singaporeans. Dr Koh obtained a Bachelor of Arts (1988) from the National University of Singapore, a master's degree (1990) in Third World Studies at the Department of Sociological Studies, University of Sheffield, United Kingdom, and a PhD from the same institution in 1995 and joined the Institute of Policy Studies in the following year.

LEE Hsien Loong was sworn in as Singapore's third Prime Minister on 12 August 2004. Mr Lee was first elected Member of Parliament (MP) in 1984 as a candidate of the People's Action Party (PAP) and has been re-elected six times, most recently in 2011 as an MP for the Ang Mo Kio Group Representation Constituency. He was elected to the Central Executive Committee of the PAP in 1986, and became its Secretary-General in 2004. Mr Lee was appointed Minister of State in the Ministry of Trade and Industry (MTI) and the Ministry of Defence in 1984. He was became a full Minister for Trade and Industry in 1987, and was concurrently Second Minister for Defence. In 1990, Mr Lee was appointed Deputy Prime Minister with responsibilities in economic and civil service matters. He concurrently served as Chairman of the Monetary Authority of Singapore (MAS) from 1998 until 2004, and Minister for Finance from 2001 until 2007. Mr Lee was appointed Chairman of Government of Singapore Investment Corporation (GIC) in June 2011. Mr Lee also chairs the Research, Innovation and Enterprise Council (RIEC), an international panel to oversee Singapore's major effort in promoting research and development. Before entering politics, Mr Lee was a Brigadier-General in the Singapore Armed Forces (SAF). He attended the US Army Command and General Staff College at Fort Leavenworth, Kansas, and held various staff and command posts, including the Director of the Joint Operations and Plans Directorate, and Chief of Staff of the General Staff. Mr Lee was born on 10 February 1952 and completed his schooling in Singapore. He studied at the University of Cambridge, graduating with a BA in Mathematics and a Diploma in Computer Science. He subsequently earned a Master in Public Administration from the Harvard Kennedy School.

LEE Tzu Yang is a member of the Academic Panel of the Institute of Policy Studies and a member of the governing board of the Institute before it became part of the Lee Kuan Yew School of Public Policy. He graduated from the London School of Economics and Political Science in 1976 and joined Shell in 1979. He has worked in a variety of roles, businesses and countries and is now Chairman of Shell Companies in Singapore. Previously a member of the board of trustees of the National University of Singapore and the National Arts Council, he is currently a member of the advisory board of the Centre for Liveable Cities and chairs the School of the Arts, and the Workplace Safety and Health Council. He is a member of the Legal Service Commission and was recently appointed to the Council of Presidential Advisers. In 2005, he worked on the Singapore Green Plan on the subject of water. From 2004–2010, he chaired the Water Network of people, private and public interests in water. He has an interest in arts and education and led the study on the Specialised Arts School in 2003 and the Arts and Culture Strategic Review in 2010–2011.

Sylvia LIM was elected as the Member of Parliament (MP) for the Aljunied Group Representation Constituency (Serangoon Division) in the 2011 General Election. She is also the Chairman of the Workers' Party. Prior to the election, she was a Non-Constituency Member of Parliament for five years. Ms Lim holds a Bachelor of Law (Hons) degree from the National University of Singapore and obtained a Master of Law in 1989 from the University of London. She was called to the Singapore Bar in 1991. That year, she joined the Singapore Police Force as a Police Inspector where she served for three years. In 1994, she returned to practise law in the private sector, with M/s Lim & Lim. In 1998 she joined Temasek Polytechnic as a law lecturer and from 2004 to 2011, she was concurrently Manager of Professional Development at the Polytechnic's Business School overseeing its adult education. Ms Lim is currently a Senior Associate at M/s Peter Low LLC, a local law firm, and is pursuing a Master of Science with Michigan State University in the field of criminal justice.

Donald LOW is Senior Fellow and Assistant Dean of Research Centres at the Lee Kuan Yew School of Public Policy of the National University of Singapore. Prior to his current appointment, Mr Low served 15 years in the Singapore government. During that time, he established the Centre for Public Economics in the Civil Service College of Singapore in 2009. The centre's mission is to advance economics literacy in the Singapore government. He was the Director of Fiscal Policy at the Ministry of Finance from 2004 to 2005 and the Director of the Strategic Policy Office in the Public Service Division from 2006 to 2007. Mr Low recently co-wrote and edited *Behavioural Economics and Policy Design: Examples from Singapore* (2011), a pioneering book that details how the Singapore government has applied ideas from the field of behavioural economics in the design of public policies. Mr Low holds a double first in Politics, Philosophy and Economics from Oxford University and a Master in International Public Policy from Johns Hopkins University's School of Advanced International Studies. He is currently a Vice President at the Economics Society of Singapore.

Kishore MAHBUBANI is the Dean and Professor in the Practice of Public Policy at the Lee Kuan Yew School of Public Policy of the National University of Singapore. He has enjoyed a career in government and, at the same time, has written extensively on public issues. He was with the Singapore Foreign Service for 33 years (1971–2004) where he had postings in Cambodia, Malaysia, Washington DC and New York. In New York, he served two postings as Singapore's Ambassador to the UN and as President of the UN Security Council (2001 and 2002). He was Permanent Secretary at the Foreign Ministry from 1993–1998. Currently, he is in the world of ideas and has spoken at various high-level international conferences and published globally. He recently launched *The Great Convergence: Asia, the West,* and his next book, *The Logic of One World* is due to be published soon.

NIZAM Ismail is Chairman of the Centre for Research on Islamic and Malay Affairs (RIMA). He was the immediate past Chairman of the Association of Muslim Professionals (AMP) and remains a board member at the Association. He was also the Chairman of AMP's Convention Steering Committee for 3rd Convention of Muslim Professionals. An Advocate and Solicitor, Mr Nizam graduated from National University of Singapore's Law School. He has assumed various senior roles in legal and compliance in the financial sector.

Lawrence WONG was elected as the Member of Parliament for the West Coast Group Representation Constituency (Boon Lay Division) in the 2011 General Election. He was appointed the Acting Minister for Culture, Community and Youth on 1 Nov 2012, and is concurrently the Senior Minister of State at the Ministry of Communications and Information. He is also a member of the Board of Directors of the Monetary Authority of Singapore. Mr Wong spent his earlier professional life as a civil servant, with stints in the Energy Market Authority, the Prime Minister's Office, the Ministry of Health and the Ministry of Finance. He obtained his undergraduate and master's degrees in Economics from the University of Wisconsin-Madison and the University of Michigan-Ann Arbor. He also has a Master in Public Administration from the Harvard Kennedy School.

www.ingramcontent.com/pod-product-compliance
Lightning Source LLC
Chambersburg PA
CBHW070351270326
41926CB00017B/4081